Lectures on Jung's Typology

SEMINAR SERIES

Interpretative commentaries edited from lecture courses. Suitable for study groups, libraries, and the private reader.

LECTURES ON
Jung's Typology

Marie-Louise von Franz
The Inferior Function

James Hillman
The Feeling Function

Spring Publications, Inc.
Dallas, Texas

Published by Spring Publications, Inc.; P.O. Box 222069; Dallas, Texas 75222
Printed in the United States of America

International distributors:
Spring; Postfach; 8803 Rüschlikon; Switzerland.
Japan Spring Sha, Inc.; 12–10, 2-Chome, Nigawa Takamaru;
    Takarazuka 665, Japan.
Element Books Ltd; Longmead Shaftesbury; Dorset SP7 8PL; England.
Astam Books Pty. Ltd.; 27B Llewellyn St.; Balmain, Sydney, N.S.W. 2041; Australia.
Libros e Imagenes; Apdo. Post 40–085; México D.F. 06140; México.

Cover design and production by Patricia Mora and Maribeth Lipscomb

Library of Congress Cataloging-in-Publication Data

Lectures on Jung's typology.

  (Seminar series ; 4)
  Corrected printing.
  Bibliography: p.
  Contents: The inferior function / Marie-Louise von
Franz—The feeling function / James Hillman.
  1. Typology (Psychology) 2. Emotions.
3. Complexes (Psychology) 4. Jung, C. G. (Carl Gustav),
1875–1961—Contributions in typology. I. Franz, Marie-
Louise von, 1915–   . Inferior function. 1986.
II. Hillman, James. Feeling function. 1986.
III. Series: Seminar series (Spring Publications, Inc.)
; 4.
BF698.3.L43 1986   155.2'64   86–17912
ISBN 0–88214–104X

CONTENTS

ACKNOWLEDGMENTS

My four chapters in this volume were presented as a series of lectures at the C. G. Jung Institute, Zürich, during the Winter Semester, January 1961. The organization of the chapters departs slightly from the lectures; questions and answers have been grouped together, and the editors have here and there re-arranged material into appropriate chapters.

I wish to thank Una Thomas whose faithful typescript provides the basis of these chapters. For the final form in which this seminar now appears I wish to thank Murray Stein for the editing.

Marie-Louise von Franz
January 1971

The following chapters result from lectures given during the years 1962 and 1963 in London, Boston and Houston on "Feeling," and then at the C. G. Jung Institute, Zürich, Summer Semester, 1966, on "The Feeling Function." I have revised them for this publication. Eleanor Mattern recorded and typed the manuscript on which the revision is based. Margit van Leight Frank read through the first typescript and made some helpful suggestions.

James Hillman
October 1970

PART ONE

Marie-Louise von Franz
The Inferior Function

CHAPTER I

A General Characterization
of the Inferior Function

Psychological Types is one of Jung's earliest books. When he wrote it, he was in many respects struggling in the dark. Since the book was written, the idea of the four functions of consciousness, and the functioning of the conscious human personality in this fourfold way, has proved tremendously productive. The idea of the four functions evolved in Jung's thought and even turned up in the religious problem of the three and the four.

For those who are unfamiliar with this field, I must give a brief sketch of the pattern of the four functions in Jungian psychology. Jung first differentiated two attitudinal types: the extravert and the introvert. In the extravert the conscious libido habitually flows toward the object, but there is an unconscious secret counter-action back toward the subject. In the case of the introvert, the opposite occurs: he feels as if an overwhelming object wants constantly to affect him, from which he has continually to retire; everything is falling upon him, he is constantly overwhelmed by impressions, but he is unaware that he is secretly borrowing psychic energy from and lending it to the object through his unconscious extraversion.

EXTRAVERTED TYPE   INTROVERTED TYPE

This diagram represents the difference between the extravert and the introvert. The four functions—sensation, thinking, feeling and intuition—each of which can be extraverted or introverted, produce eight types: extraverted thinking, introverted thinking; extraverted feeling, introverted feeling, etc.

I am assuming you know about the arrangement of the functions—namely, that the two rational functions, thinking and feeling, are opposite each other, as are the two irrational functions, sensation and intuition:

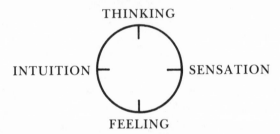

The question has often been raised: why on earth should there be four functions? Why not three? Or five? That cannot be answered theoretically; it is simply a question of checking facts and of seeing whether one can find more or fewer functions and another typology. For Jung it was a great discovery when he later found confirmation of his more intuitively conceived idea in the fact that everywhere in myths and religious symbolism there appears the model of the fourfold structure of the psyche. In studying the behavior of his patients, he found that he had apparently hit upon a basic structure. Naturally, the basic fourfold structure of the psyche, which means more than only the conscious functions, is generally represented as a purely primitive self-manifestation of the unconscious, usually as an undifferentiated quaternion. There are just four principles of more or less the same kind: four colors, or angles, or gods, etc. The more they are connected with consciousness, the more they tend to become three animals and one human being, or three good gods and one evil god. One also finds those more differentiated mandalas where the four poles of the quaternary structure are different from each other, particularly if the material has been consciously worked upon a great deal. There one often finds the classic problem of the three and the four about which Jung has written so much. This means that when, from this basic structure, one or the other functions becomes conscious, or where under optimum conditions three functions become conscious, this has the effect of also changing the basic structure of the psyche. Neither in psychology nor in any other field of reality is there ever a one-sided course of action, for if the unconscious builds up a field of consciousness, the repercussion of such a change produces an alteration in the unconscious structure as well. Therefore when one finds in dreams and mythological material that this basic structure appears in an altered form, it can be concluded that a part of the problem of the functions has already become conscious, and, due to the counter-action, even the basic structure of the psyche has a changed or modified form.

The differentiation of types starts in very early childhood. For instance, the two attitudes—extravert and introvert—can actually be seen in a child of one or one-and-a-half, though perhaps not always very clearly. Jung once told of the case of a child who would not enter a room before it had been told the names of the pieces of furniture there—table, chair, etc. That is typical of a definitely introverted attitude, where the object is terrifying and has to be banished or put in its place by a word, a propitiating gesture by which the object is made known and cannot misbehave. In such little details, if you know how to look for them, you can observe the tendency toward introversion or extraversion in a very small child.

The functions, naturally, do not show so early, but by the kindergarten age one can usually observe the development of a main function by a preference for some occupation or by the child's behavior toward another child. Children, like adults, tend to do frequently what they can do well and to avoid the things which they cannot do well. Probably most people do as I did with my school work: I was gifted in mathematics and did that first, leaving whatever I was not good at till the end. The natural tendency is to defer doing, or to push off on other people, the thing in which one does not feel superior. By such natural behavior, the one-sidedness is increased more and more. Then comes the family attitude: the boy who is very intelligent must study later on, or the child gifted in practical matters must become an engineer. The surroundings reinforce the existing one-sided tendencies, the so-called 'gifts,' and there is thus an increase in the development of the superior function and a slow degeneration of the other side of the personality. This is an unavoidable process and even has great advantages. Many people fit into this pattern, and one can tell their type at once; others may be very difficult to define.

Some people have trouble in finding out their own type, which very often is due to the fact that they are distorted types. This is not a very frequent occurrence, but it does happen in cases where someone would naturally have become a feeling type or an intuitive, but was forced by the surrounding atmosphere to develop another function. Suppose a boy is born a feeling type in an intellectually ambitious family. His surroundings will exert pressure upon him to become an intellectual, and his original predisposition as a feeling type will be thwarted or despised. Usually, in such a case, he is unable to become a thinking type: that would be one step too far. But he might well develop sensation or intuition, one of the auxiliary functions, so as to be relatively better adapted to his surroundings; his main function is simply 'out' in the milieu in which he grows up.

Distorted types have advantages and disadvantages. The disadvantage is that from the very beginning they cannot develop their main disposition; they therefore remain a bit below the mark they would have reached had they developed in the one-sided way. On the other hand, they have been forced ahead of time into doing something which in the second half of life they would have had to do anyway. In analysis, one can very often help people switch back to the original type, and they are then able to pick up the other function very quickly and reach a developed stage, for the original disposition is a help in that direction. They are like fish which can now return happily to the water.

Another aspect of the early stages, when one is still developing one's main function, is the tendency in families to distribute the functions: one member is the family introvert, another becomes the family's practical engineer, a third the family's seer and prophet and so on. The others happily give up this function because one member can do it so much better. This sets up vital groups which function well, and individuals only get into trouble when the group falls apart. There is a very strong tendency in most families, and also in other groups, to solve the function problem by distributing the functions and relying on the superior function of the other.

In marriage, as Jung points out, one tends to marry the opposite type, and then again he is, or so he thinks for the moment, freed from the disagreeable task of confronting his own inferior function. That is one of the great blessings and sources of happiness in the early stages of a marriage; suddenly the whole weight of the inferior function is gone, one lives in a blessed oneness with the other, and every problem is solved! But if one of the partners dies, or the need comes up in one of them to develop the inferior function instead of just leaving those sections of life to the other, the trouble starts. The same happens again in the choice of analysts. Frequently people choose the opposite type as analyst because, for instance, the feeling type cannot think and so admires tremendously a person who can. This course is not to be recommended, because if one is always with someone who knows it all he gets discouraged and gives up completely. He might feel very happy because now thinking is taken care of, but this is not an adequate solution. Jung, for instance, always liked to send people with the same blind spots to each other because, he said, if two idiots sit together and neither can think they will get into such trouble that at least one of them will begin to think! It would, of course, be the same with the other functions: they just sit there and hope that the other will do the work. If one goes to the opposite type, something to be borne in mind, especially by the analyst, is to be very careful not to display the superior function too much. One must, against one's real feeling, constantly pretend that one does not know, or feels incapable—has no idea—and so on. One has to give up the superior function in order not to paralyze the first shy attempts the analysand might make in this field.

If we ask what determines the original basic disposition, the answer is that we don't know! Jung, at the end of *Psychological Types*, says that it has probably a biological parallel. He points out, for instance, the two ways in which animal species adapt to reality: either by propagating tremendously and having an inferior defense mechanism—for example, fleas, lice and rabbits —or by having few offspring and building up tremendous defense mechanisms, as for instance the hedgehog or the elephant. Thus already in nature there are two possibilities for dealing with reality: either you defend yourself against it, keeping it off while building your own life, or you pour yourself into it and overcome or conquer it. That would be introverted and extraverted functioning in the biological realm.

I think one may go even further. When Jung brought out his book on types, not much had been published on animal behavior, but in the modern books one can see that among the animals there is a *mixtum compositum* of factors in most patterns of behavior. Thus some aspects of animal behavior come more from within—that is, they come into play without any outer stimulus—while other animal behavior depends more on outer stimuli. Heinrich Hediger, Professor of Zoology at Zürich University and Director of the Zürich Zoo, has said in recent lectures that the higher anthropoid apes are incapable of performing the sexual acts unless they have observed another ape and learned in that way, whereas with many other animals it is quite the opposite: without ever having seen animals of their species mating, the urge from within is sufficient. But if in a zoo the higher apes are brought up without ever seeing a companion mate, they remain ignorant and incompetent, just as a human being does. Therefore it is obvious that the behavior of an animal depends in part on an outer factor and is in part conditioned by an inborn disposition. The behavior pattern is a result of a mutual interaction between inner and outer factors.

Experiments have been made by incubating stork's eggs and keeping them from contact with the social group. When birds

Storks

produced from such eggs are released, those bred of eggs whose group fly over Yugoslavia to Africa will fly over that country, and those produced from the eggs of birds which fly over Spain will fly over Spain to Africa. This proves that they rely completely on an inborn disposition that tells them how to reach Africa. But if a stork bred from the Yugoslav group is put with the birds which fly over Spain, the bird will fly with them and not follow his inborn disposition. This shows the two possibilities very clearly—being influenced by outer factors and social pressure, or simply following the inborn disposition. To study the pre-forms of the attitude type in the results of what has now been found out about animal behavior would afford an interesting subject for an Institute student's thesis, for if we ask how such dispositions originated in man, we have to look back to animal life after this manner.

I would like now to characterize the inferior function in its general behavior. You can say that all superior functions have a tendency to behave in a certain way; the inferior function, too, irrespective of which it may be, has a general type of behavior. The behavior of the inferior function is wonderfully mirrored in those fairy tales where there is the following structure. A king has three sons. He likes the two elder sons, but the youngest is regarded as a fool. The king then sets a task in which the sons may have to find the water of life, or the most beautiful bride, or chase away a secret enemy who every night steals the horses or the golden apples out of the royal garden. Generally, the two elder sons set out and get nowhere or get stuck, and then the third saddles his horse while everybody laughs and tells him he'd better stay at home by the stove where he belongs. But it is he who usually performs the great task.

This fourth figure—the third son, but the fourth figure in the setup—has, according to the myths, different superficial qualities. Sometimes he is the youngest, sometimes he is a bit idiotic, and sometimes he is a complete fool. There are different versions, but he is always in some such category. In a beautiful Russian fairy tale, for instance, he is looked upon as a complete idiot. The two elder sons ride out from their father's stable on wonderful horses, but the youngest takes a little shaggy pony and sits on it the wrong way round—with his head toward the horse's tail—and goes off, derided by everybody. He is, of course, Ivan, the Russian hero, and the one who inherits the kingdom. Then there are the themes of the cripple and of the soldier who has deserted or has been wounded and discharged from the army and who is lost in the woods. Or there may be a poor peasant boy who becomes king.

In all these cases, one knows from the very beginning of the story that it concerns something more than the four functions, for the fool is an archetypal religious figure, embracing more than only the inferior function. He implies a part of the human personality, or even of humanity, which remained behind and therefore still has the original wholeness of nature. He symbolizes a specific, mainly religious, function. But in mythology, as soon as the fool appears as the fourth in a group of four people, we have a certain right to assume that he mirrors the general behavior of an inferior function. I have often tried, in interpreting fairy tales, to go further into detail and to call the king the thinking and the fourth son the feeling function, but in my experience that does not work. One has to twist the material and play some dishonest tricks to force the issues like this. So I have come to the conclusion that we cannot go that far, but must just say that in mythology such a third son, or such a fool, simply represents the general behavior of an inferior function, whichever it may be. It is neither individual nor specific, but a general outline.

If one studies individual cases, one can see that the inferior function tends to behave after the manner of such a 'fool' hero, the divine fool or idiot hero. He represents the despised part of the personality, the ridiculous and unadapted part, but also that part which builds up the connection with the unconscious and therefore holds the secret key to the unconscious totality of the person.

One can say that the inferior function always makes the bridge to the unconscious. It is always directed toward the unconscious and the symbolic world. But that is not to say that it is directed either to the inside or the outside; this varies individually. For instance, an introverted thinking type has an inferior extraverted feeling function; its movement will be toward outer objects, to other people, but such people will have a symbolic meaning for the person, being carriers of symbols of the unconscious. The symbolic meaning of an unconscious fact appears outside, as the quality of the outer object. If an introvert, with his habitual way of introjecting, says he need not telephone Mrs. So-and-So—she is just the symbol of his anima and therefore symbolic, and the actual person does not matter for it only happened that his projection falls there—then he will never get to the bottom of his inferior function. He will never assimilate it as a problem because the feeling of an introverted thinking type is generally genuinely extraverted. By such a trick he simply tries to catch hold of his inferior function by means of his superior function and pull it inside. He introjects at the wrong moment so as to maintain the predominance of his superior over his inferior function. An introvert who wants to assimilate his inferior function must relate to outer objects, bearing in mind that they are symbolic. He must not, however, draw the conclusion that they are *only* symbolic and that, therefore, outer objects can be dispensed with. That is a lousy, dishonest trick which many introverts play with their inferior function. Naturally extraverts do the same thing, only the other way round. Therefore it must not be said that the inferior function is always directed inward. It is directed toward the unconscious, whether it appears on the inside or the outside, and it is always the carrier of symbolic experiences which may come from within or without.

To the general outline of the inferior function belongs the fact that it is generally slow, in contrast to the superior function. Jung calls it infantile and tyrannical. We have to go into this in detail. One of the great troubles of the inferior function is its slowness, which is one reason why people hate to start work on it; the reaction of the superior function comes out quickly and well adapted, while many people have no idea where their inferior function really is. For instance, thinking types have no idea whether they have feeling or what kind of feeling it is. They have to sit half an hour and meditate as to whether they have feelings about something and, if so, what they are. If you ask a thinking type what he feels, he generally either replies with a thought or gives a quick conventional reaction; and if you then insist on knowing what he really feels, he does not know. Pulling it up from his belly, so to speak, can take half an hour. Or, if an intuitive fills out a tax form he needs a week where other people would take a day. He simply cannot do it, or if he is to do it accurately and in the right way he takes forever. I know an introverted intuitive woman—and to go with her to choose a blouse! Never again! It takes an eternity, until the whole shop is mad! But it cannot be speeded up. It does not help to get impatient. And naturally that is what is so discouraging about getting up the inferior function: one has not the time for it.

This cannot be helped. It is a stage which cannot be skipped. If people lose patience and say 'to hell with it,' it means they give up. That is hopeless, for it simply means that they cut the fourth function out and replace it by some kind of artificial mechanism—by a crutch. It cannot be speeded up, or only to a small extent; it can never achieve the speed of the superior function. It is this way for very good reasons. If you think of the turning point of life and the problems of aging and of turning within, then this slowing down of the whole life process by bringing in the inferior function is just the thing which is needed. So the slowness should not be treated with impatience and with trying to educate 'the damned inferior function'; one should rather accept the fact that in this realm one has to waste time. That is just the value of it, because that gives the unconscious a chance to come in.   *BRIDGE*

Another typical aspect of the inferior function, which is also connected with its unadaptedness and primitiveness, is its touchiness and tyranny. Most people, when their inferior function is in any way touched upon, become terribly childish: they can't stand the slightest criticism and always feel attacked. Here they are uncertain of themselves; with that, naturally, they tyrannize everybody around them because everybody has to walk carefully. If you want to say something about another person's inferior function, it is like walking on eggs; people cannot stand any criticism there. A *rîte d'entrée* is required. One must wait for the right moment, for a peaceful atmosphere, and then carefully, with a long introductory speech, one might get across some slight criticism about the inferior function.

But simply to shoot criticism at people will only get them absolutely bewildered and emotional, and the situation is ruined. I learned this for the first time with amazement many years ago when I was still studying. A fellow student showed me a paper she had written. She was a feeling type. The paper was very good, but in a minor passage where she switched from one theme to another it seemed to me that there was a hiatus in the connection of thought. What she said was quite right, but between the two passages, for a thinking type, the logical transition was lacking. So I said to her that I thought it was an excellent paper but that on one page she might make a better transition. At that, she got absolutely emotional and said: "Oh well, then it's all ruined, I shall just burn it," and she grabbed it out of my hand saying: "I know it's junk, I shall burn it up!" I pulled it from her: "For God's sake, don't burn it up!" "Oh well," she said, "I knew you thought it would be junk," and in this vein she went on and on. When the storm was over I was able to get in a word and said: "You need not even retype it, you only need to write in one little sentence to make the transition—just one sentence between these two paragraphs." The storm started all over again, and I gave up!

I saw her later, and she told me that the night afterward she dreamt that her house burnt down and, typically, the fire started in the roof! I thought: "My God, these feeling types!" For her, writing the paper had been such an achievement, bringing out some thoughts, and it had been just at the limit of what she could do. She simply couldn't stand that little bit. It wasn't even criticism, but just the idea that it could be improved a bit. That is an extreme case of what happens with the inferior function. It tyrannizes its surroundings by being touchy, for all touchiness is a form of secret tyranny. Sensitive people are just tyrannical people: everybody else has to adapt to them instead of their trying to adapt to others. But people who are well adapted still generally have a kind of childish, touchy spot where one cannot talk to them reasonably, and one has to adopt bush manners as if dealing with tigers and elephants.

In Van Gennep's *Les Rîtes de Passage* one finds examples of how explorers approach a primitive village. They have to stop several miles away, and then three messengers from the village come; the villagers have to be assured that the explorers have no evil designs and especially that they do not intend to use black

Kinship ritual

magic against the inhabitants. The messengers then go back, and when they return gifts are exchanged. Sometimes even women are exchanged, or they may be given to the guests who sleep with them, because that establishes a kind of kinship. If a man sleeps with another's wife he is kin to him; he has been taken into his family. The Naskapi Indians on the Labrador peninsula, for example, do that, and many Eskimos lend their wives to foreigners for the night. This is to prevent any kind of evil explosion, any chance that a guest might murder the people in the house, or that the latter might murder the guest. Many primitive people, also, cut each other and exchange blood. There is also a special way of kissing and of exchanging gifts. All those *rîtes de passage* come into play as soon as you have to relate to people on the level of the inferior function.

One can see the same thing in everyday life. For instance, one may have known someone for two or three years, but only on the conventional level of having tea or dinner together and talking about the weather and politics and theoretical questions, but never having dared to touch the sore spots in each other or having brought the conversation round to some ticklish point. But then one day one feels that it is not a real relationship, that one is not getting really close. Then there is a little wine, and if the atmosphere is favorable the sore spots come out and one invites the other to come out with his. So, through all the precautions of bush politeness, two persons slowly really approach. I don't know any other formula than bush politeness. That is the formula with which to approach the other side, for the sore spots generally are connected with the inferior function.

There is a difference between personal politeness and bush politeness. Let's take a practical example. I was once driving with a man, an intuitive type. We were driving home late at night, and he forgot to turn on the ignition. He tried over and over again to start the car and it would not go. I ventured politely to ask whether he had switched the ignition on? "Naturally," came the reply, but with such an affect that I did not dare say any more! Now that was his inferior sensation! So there we sat for half an hour, and I felt sure of what the trouble was but didn't know how to tell him. The slightest tone of knowing better would have produced an explosion. I felt so helpless that I actually tried to get to a garage. I even looked at the water, but knew all the time what was wrong and didn't know how to get round the sore spot. There was the question of his prestige. I must add that a lot of alcohol contributed to the *abaissement,* which made the affects that much more explosive. Then, too, the man was older than I, and there was the question of being impolite. But it isn't the persona; it is another kind of politeness. It is rather a matter of having real feeling and understanding for the other person's weakness and not daring to touch it.

The inferior function and the sore spot are absolutely connected. If he had not had inferior sensation, he would not have been so touchy. If I had said, "Have you switched on?" he would have replied, "Oh, my God!" and done so, and off we would have gone. But instead we sat for an hour on the road guessing what the trouble could be, and I just did not know how to approach this sore area of the inferior function.

These examples also illustrate another general feature of the inferior function: namely, a tremendous charge of emotion is generally connected with its processes. As soon as you get into this realm people easily become emotional. In the example you can see the negative side of this connection to the emotions, but there is also a very positive aspect. In the realm of the inferior function there is a great concentration of life, so that as soon as the superior function is worn out—begins to rattle and lose oil like an old car—if people succeed in turning to their inferior function they will rediscover a new potential of life. Everything in the realm of the inferior function becomes exciting, dramatic, full of positive and negative possibilities. There is tremendous tension and the world is, as it were, rediscovered through the inferior function. But the disadvantage of turning to the inferior function is that it has this unadapted aspect. That is why in the fairy tales which I mentioned it is the fool, the third son of the group of four royal people, who can find the water of life or the great treasure. The inferior function brings a renewal of life if one allows it to come up in its own realm.

Many people discover relatively soon in life that the realm of their inferior function is where they are emotional, touchy and unadapted, and they therefore acquire the habit of covering up this part of their personality with a surrogate pseudo-reaction.

For instance, a thinking type often cannot express his feelings normally and in the appropriate manner at the right time. It can happen that when he hears that the husband of a friend has died he cries, but when he meets the widow not a word of pity will come out. They not only look very cold, but they really do not feel anything! They had all the feeling before, when at home, but now in the appropriate situation they cannot pull it out. Thinking types are very often looked on by other people as having no feeling; this is absolutely not true. It is not that they have no feeling but that they cannot express it at the appropriate moment. They have the feeling somehow and somewhere, but not just when they ought to produce it. It is a great error, also, to assume that feeling types cannot think. They think very well, and very often have deep, good and genuine thoughts, unconventional thoughts, but they come and go as they like. For instance, it is very difficult for a feeling type to pull up his right kind of thinking during an exam. There he ought to think, but thinking just goes! As soon as he is at home he can think again, but his thinking does not comply, is not amiable enough to come up at the right time. He is looked upon by society as being stupid because he cannot produce his thinking at will.

Life has no mercy with the inferiority of the inferior function. That is why people produce such 'covering up' reactions. Because it is not their real reaction, they simply borrow from the collective. A feeling type, when pressed for thinking reactions, loves to serve up a lot of commonplace remarks or thoughts which are not his real thoughts, but he has to think quickly and the real thought is not yet up to the level at which it can be expressed. So they just make a few commonplace remarks or, what is very usual for feeling types, they use material they have learnt by heart. The same is true for thinking types who get into the habit of producing a kind of amiable, conventional feeling. They send flowers, bring chocolate, or make some very conventional expression of feeling. For example, I have drawn up a form letter of condolence with certain phrases which have struck me as being very nice and touching. If I tried to express my real feelings, I would stick at such a letter for three days! So in all these situations I make a cocktail of the conventional phrases I have collected through my life. The same applies to intuitives with their inferior sensation; they simply have the habitual, technical ways of dealing with it, borrowing help from the collective. One must not be deceived by these adaptive reactions if one tries to connect with another person. You can always observe these 'covering up' reactions by the fact that they are impersonal and banal and very collective. They have no convincing personal quality about them.

In examining the dynamic interplay between the functions, one must always recognize the hold which the superior function has on the inferior. When someone tries to meet his inferior function and experiences emotional shock or pain in confronting its real reactions, then the superior function at once says: "Ah, that is something, now we must organize that." The superior function, like an eagle seizing a mouse, tries to get hold of the inferior function and bring it over into its own realm. I know a natural scientist, a very successful, introverted thinking type, who in his fifties became very bored with his professional work and began roaming about looking for other possibilities. His wife and family could have told him a lot about his inferior feeling, a field for experimentation right under his nose. He had several dreams of collecting rare mountain flowers, which clearly showed what the unconscious was now aiming at. He had the typical inferior feeling of the thinking type, namely, rare and very special feeling. The flowers in the mountains have a much more intense color than those of the plains, and this is also typical for the inferior feeling of a thinking type. He thought he had a good idea for a hobby, so he made friends with a botanist and went off for days, all through his holidays, collecting mountain flowers. Any attempts made by other people at telling him that he could do something about his feeling function only met with the reply that he had given up his main function and *was* doing something with his other side. He was studying mountain flowers! Thus he got stuck in the concretistic interpretation instead of taking the dream symbolically, and he made a sort of science of it. He wanted knowledge of those flowers, so the main function was at it again, and the inferior function once more was frustrated.

To take an irrational type: there is the intuitive who gets into a situation where he should use his inferior sensation. He becomes attracted by the idea of stone-cutting or working with clay. This sort of thing very often helps inferior sensation come up in intuitives, for by such means they may get in touch with outer purpose or reason, with some kind of concrete material, with matter. He will, perhaps, mold something in clay—say, a very helpless looking, childish statue of an animal. Then he experiences something improving in himself, but immediately —like an eagle—intuition pounces on it and says: "This is it, that's what should be introduced into all the schools," and away he goes into his intuition again, into all the possibilities of clay molding, what could be done with it in the education of humanity, what it would include, and how it is the key to the experience of the godhead. The intuitive always brings in the whole world. But the one thing that is not considered is the molding of another figure! The main function is raving again. Having had this quickening and vivifying touch with the earth, off it goes, up into the air again. The same thing happens with the feeling type who, when cornered by absolute necessity, sometimes produces a few thoughts. Then he quickly escapes this hot bath and never returns to it, but he has a feeling judgment about what thinking is like and the uses it has and so on. He makes a number of evaluations instead of continuing the process. In this way the superior function tries to get hold of the inferior function and organize it.

Another aspect of the dynamic interplay of the functions is the way in which the inferior function intrudes into the superior and falsifies it. There was a marvelous demonstration of this some time ago in the case of a certain Professor K. who made an attack on the psychology of the unconscious in the *Neue Zürcher Zeitung.* He is a pupil of Heidegger and an absolute demonstration of overworked introverted thinking. This has the unfortunate effect of his being unable to assert anything more than that life is an ontological phenomenon of existence. He enriches his statement with a few more impressive adjectives, but that is what it amounts to. This one thought, that "existence really exists," expresses a divine plenitude for him, as it also did for Parmenides. He cannot cease reassuring us about such existence. Then he says: "But the unconscious would be an uncanny theater of marionettes and ghosts." There you have an excellent illustration of what Jung means when he says: "The unconscious fantasy becomes proportionately enriched by a multitude of archaically formed facts, a veritable pandemonium of magical factors." That is exactly what Professor K. expounds in his article—the idea of the unconscious is awful, it is just a theatrical pandemonium—and then he saves his conscious position by asserting that it simply doesn't exist: it is just an invention of the psychologists! If you overdo one of the conscious attitudes it becomes poor and loses fertility; also, the unconscious counter-function, the opposite, encroaches upon the main function and falsifies it. That is obvious in Professor K.'s article; it shows that his feeling is really concerned with enlightening mankind as to the absurdity of the idea of the psychology of the unconscious. He entirely loses the objective style to which we are accustomed in scientific discussion and feels himself to be a prophet whose mission it is to save mankind from some evil poison. His whole moral, or feeling, function came up and contaminated his thinking. His thinking became subjective instead of objective, and it was obvious that he had not read the literature on the psychology of the unconscious.

Another way in which the inferior function often intrudes upon the superior can be shown in the case of a very down-to-earth, realistic, introverted sensation type. Sensation types, whether introverted or extraverted, are generally quite good in their relationship to money, in not being too extravagant. But if such a type overdoes this, his inferior intuition becomes involved. I knew a sensation type who became madly stingy and could practically not move about in life any longer because —well, in Switzerland everything costs something! When one tried to find out where this sudden stinginess originated —hitherto he had been just moderately stingy like most people here—one noticed that he produced any number of dark possibilities in life: he might have an accident and be unable to work and support his family; something might happen to his family; his wife might have a long illness; his son might fail in his studies and need more years than usual; his mother-in-law, a very rich woman, might suddenly get furious with him and leave her money to another family instead of his, etc. Those are instances of the dark fears of what might happen. This is typical of negative inferior intuition. Only the dark possibilities are envisaged. The first appearances of his inferior intuition reinforced his sensation in the wrong way by making him stingy. Life no longer flowed because everything was falsified by the invasion of inferior intuition.

When the time comes for the development of the other functions, there are generally two associated phenomena: the superior function degenerates like an old car which begins to run down and get worn out, and the ego becomes bored with it because everything you can do too well becomes boring; then, the inferior function, instead of appearing in its own field, tends to invade the main function, giving it an unadapted, neurotic twist. You are thus confronted with a neurotic *mixtum compositum*—a thinking type who can't think any longer or a feeling type who doesn't show any agreeable feeling any more. There is a transitional stage where people are neither fish, nor flesh, nor good red herring! Formerly they were good thinkers, but they can't think any more and they have not yet reached a new level. It is therefore very important to know one's type and recognize what the unconscious is up to now, for otherwise one is caught from behind.

One of the great difficulties in defining one's own or another person's type occurs when people have already reached the stage of being bored with their main function and their main attitude. They very often assure you with absolute sincerity that they belong to the type opposite from what they really are. The extravert swears that he is deeply introverted, and vice versa. This comes from the fact that the inferior function subjectively feels itself to be the real one; it feels itself the most important, most genuine attitude. So, a thinking type, because he knows that everything in his life matters from the feeling aspect, will assure you that he is a feeling type. It does no good, therefore, to think of what matters *most* when trying to discover one's type; rather ask: "What do I habitually do most?" An extravert can be constantly extraverting but will assure you, and will mean it, that he is deeply introverted and only concerned with the inner thing. That is not a swindle; it is how he feels, for he knows that though it may be only a minute a day, that minute when he introverts is the real thing, there he is close to himself, there he is real.

In the realm of the inferior function, too, one is overwhelmed, one is unhappy, one has one's great problem, one is constantly impressed by things, and therefore, in a way, the intensity of life is very often much greater there, especially if the superior function is already worn out. Practically, it is most helpful when one wants to find out the type to ask, what is the greatest cross for the person? Where is his greatest suffering? Where does he feel that he always knocks his head against the obstacle and suffers hell? That generally points to the inferior function. Many people, moreover, develop two superior functions so well that it is very difficult to say whether the person is a thinking-intuitive type or an intuitive type with good thinking, for the two seem equally good. Sometimes sensation and feeling are so well developed in an individual that you would have difficulty in ascertaining which is the first. But does the intuitive-thinking person suffer more from knocking his head on sensation facts or from feeling problems? Here you can decide which is the first, and which the well developed second, function.

I shall turn now to a general consideration of the problem of assimilating the inferior function. Consciousness evolves in early childhood from the unconscious. From our point of view, the unconscious is a primary, and consciousness a secondary, fact. Therefore the unconscious totality and the structure of the total personality exist in time before the conscious personality and could be looked at in this way:

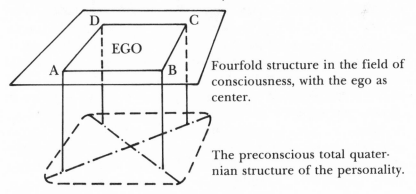

Fourfold structure in the field of consciousness, with the ego as center.

The preconscious total quaternian structure of the personality.

When the functions develop in the field of consciousness
—A B C D—there comes up from below first, let us say, the
thinking function, which then becomes one of the main functions of the ego. The ego then uses mainly the operation of
thinking in the organization of its field of consciousness. Slowly
another function appears and gradually they all—under
favorable conditions—appear in the field of consciousness.

When the fourth function comes up, however, the whole upper structure collapses. The more you pull up the fourth, the
further the upper floor descends. A mistake some people make
is that they think they can pull up the inferior function to the
level of the other conscious functions. I can only say: "Well, if
you wish to do so, try. But you can try forever!" It is absolutely
impossible to pull up—like a fisherman with his rod—the inferior function, and all such attempts as, for instance, speeding
it up or educating it to come up at the right moment prove
failures. One can try to force it to function in an exam or in certain situations in life, but this succeeds only to a certain extent
and only by bringing in conventional, borrowed material. One
cannot bring up the fourth function, for it insists on remaining
below. It is contaminated with the unconscious and remains in
that condition. Trying to fish it up would be like trying to bring
up the whole collective unconscious, which is something one
just cannot do. The fish will be too big for the rod. So what does
one do? Cut if off again? This is regression. But if you don't give
in, there is only the other alternative: the fish will pull you into
the water! At this moment comes the great conflict, which
means for the thinking type, for instance, the famous *sacrificium
intellectus* or, for the feeling type, the *sacrificium* of his feeling. It
is having the humility to go down with one's other functions to
that lower level. This, then, produces a stage between the two
layers at about the level where everything is neither thinking
nor feeling nor sensation nor intuition. Something new comes
up, namely, a completely different and new attitude toward life
in which one uses all and none of the functions all the time.

Very often someone will naively say that he is a thinking type
and is now going to develop his feeling function—what an illusion! If a person is a thinking type, he can first go either to sen-

sation or to intuition. That is his choice. Then he moves to the opposite of the two secondary functions, and lastly to the inferior one. But he cannot cross directly to the opposite function. The reason is very simple: it is that they exclude each other completely; they are incompatibles. Take the example of a staff officer who has to plan the evacuation of a town population in the best possible way under given conditions. Unfortunately his own wife and children are in the same town. If he gives in to his own feelings about them, he won't develop a good plan. He just cannot. He must simply obliterate them from his mind and tell himself that it is now his job to plan the evacuation as well as he can; he must think of his own feelings as mere sentimentality. This is a depreciation in order to free himself. One cannot make a straight jump from one function to its opposite, but one can assimilate thinking with sensation or have them functioning together. It is possible to combine the other two auxiliary functions very easily, so that in the jump from one to the other he will not suffer as much as if he had to jump to the opposite function. When one has to move from intuition to sensation one can still use the thinking function as a judge, and when intuition and sensation fight he can detach himself from the fight by thinking.

If I analyze a thinking type, I never push him into feeling at once. I see that the other functions are first assimilated to a certain extent. It is a mistake to forget this intermediary stage. Take, for instance, a thinking type who falls madly in love with a completely inappropriate person because of his inferior feeling. If he has already developed sensation, which implies a certain sense of reality, and of intuition—the capacity to smell a rat—he will not fall into complete nonsense. But if he is only a one-sided thinking type and he falls in love with an inappropriate female and has no sense of reality and of intuition, there will happen what is so beautifully depicted in the film *The Blue Angel*, where the school professor becomes a circus clown in the service of a vamp. There are no intermediary fields where he can catch himself: he is just knocked over by his inferior function. But if his analyst could see to it, while he has not yet much feeling, that at least he has developed a certain sense of reality, then he can break the difficulty with that intermediary function. I think that is something to keep in mind if one is an analyst, that one should never jump directly to the inferior function. Of course life does it; life does not care! But the analytical process should not go that way, and normally it does not do so if one follows the intimations given in the dreams. The tendency of the process is that the development should follow a serpentine movement. This is the normal way in which the unconscious tries to bring up the inferior function.

This is the end of my general outline on the problem of the inferior function. The next step will be to give a short description of what the inferior function of each type looks like in practical life.

(A period of questions and answers follows.)

Question: Why do artists tend to shy away from analysis?

Dr. von Franz: Artists often think that analysis will educate their inferior function to such an extent that it will lose its creativeness. But this is quite impossible. There is no danger, because even if the analyst should be stupid enough to try it, it cannot be done. The inferior function is a horse that cannot be educated. It is something that can be subjugated to the extent that you do not do stupid things all the time. So much is possible. I am always reminded of a story connected with my father. He bought a horse which was much too big for him: he was a small man. In the army this horse was looked upon as a criminal because one could not give it the whip. It would just bolt and throw its rider. My father fell in love with this beautiful horse and bought it, and then he made a pact with it: "I won't give you the whip if you don't throw me." That is, he dealt with it as an equal, and it became his best horse. He even won several races with it, but in cases where others would have given the whip he didn't. If he had touched it with the whip, the pact would have been finished. But the horse was intelligent, and through intensive training he could convey his wishes to it; it then did more or less what he wanted. That is the most you can accomplish with the inferior function. You can never rule or educate it and make it act as you would like, but if you are very clever and are willing to give in a lot, then you may be able to arrange so that it does not throw you. It will throw you sometimes, but not at the wrong moment.

Question: Is there a situation where functions do not differentiate one-sidedly?

Dr. von Franz: Yes. For instance, people who still live completely in nature, such as peasants and hunters and the Bushmen of whom Laurens van der Post wrote, would not survive unless they used all their functions, more or less. A peasant can never become as one-sided as a town dweller: he cannot only be an intuitive, he simply has to use his sensation; but he cannot only use that, because he has to plan the farming—when the sowing must be done and which kind of carrot or wheat must be grown, and how much, and what the prices are. Otherwise he would be ruined at once! He has also to use a certain amount of feeling because you cannot deal with your family or animals without it, and he has to have that certain smell for the weather and the future in general, without which he is always in trouble. So in natural situations things are more or less arranged so that one must, to a certain extent, use all the functions. That is why people who live under natural conditions rarely become as one-sided. This is the old, well-known problem of specialization. But among primitive peoples, too, you can see that they generally distribute the functions. For instance, my peasant neighbor always asks the fisherman who lives with him what the weather will be. He says he does not know how the fisherman can tell, but he just does, so he himself does not bother. He relies on that man's intuition and does not use his own. So even there people tend to push off certain functions on others who are better specialists. But they cannot do it as completely as town specialists do. If, for example, you are a bachelor and work in a statistical office for yourself, you really need practically no feeling! That, naturally, has its disagreeable consequences, but in nature you simply could not do that.

Question: When something is unconscious, either for the extravert or the introvert, does it always appear on the outside in its projected form?

Dr. von Franz: No. In the case of extraverts, I have seen that it very often appears within, either as a vision or a fantasy. I have often been impressed by the fact that extraverts, when they come to their other side, have a much purer relationship to the inside than the introvert. I have even been quite jealous! They have a naive and genuine and pure relationship to inner facts, for they can have a vision and take it completely seriously at once, quite naively. In an introvert, it is always distorted by his extraverted shadow who throws doubts on it. It can be said that if an extravert falls into his introversion, it will be especially genuine and especially pure and deep. Extraverts are often so proud of this that they boast loudly about what great introverts they are. They try to make it into a feather in their cap—which is typically extraverted again—and thereby ruin the whole thing. But actually, if they do not spoil it with vanity, you can see that they can have a much more childlike, naive, pure and really genuine introversion than introverts. Just as an introvert, if he wakes up to his inferior extraversion, can spread a glow of life and make life in his surroundings into a symbolic festival, better than any extravert! He can give outer life a depth of symbolic meaning and a feeling of life as a magic feast which the extravert cannot. If an extravert goes to a party he is ready to say that everybody is marvelous and, "Come on, let's get this party going!" But that is a technique and like that the party never really reaches magical depth, or very rarely; it remains on the level of the amiable surface. But if an introvert can come out with his extraversion in the right way, he can create an atmosphere where outside things become symbolic: drinking a glass of wine with a friend becomes something like a communion, and so on. But one must not forget that most people cover up their genuine inferior side with a pseudo-adaptation.

CHAPTER II

The Four Irrational Types

The Extravc•ted Sensation Type:
Inferior Introverted Intuition

The extraverted sensation type is represented in someone whose gift and specialized function is to sense and relate in a concrete and practical way to outer objects. Such people observe everything, smell everything, and on entering a room know almost at once how many people are present. Afterward, they always know whether Mrs. So-and-So was there and what dress she had on. If you put such a question to an intuitive, he would say he had not noticed and had no idea, and what *did* she have on? The sensation type is a master at noticing details.

There is the famous story of a professor of jurisprudence who tried to demonstrate to his students the unreliability of witnesses. He had two people come into the room, exchange a few sentences, and then begin to fight each other. He stopped them and said: "Now ladies and gentlemen, please write down exactly what you saw." The professor then showed that nobody was

If the extraverted sensation type is very one sided he/she will even dislike thought considering that it is getting into the abstract instead of sticking to facts.

capable of giving an exact and objective account of what had happened. They all missed certain points. Based on this staged incident, he tried to show his students that they should not rely on eye witnesses too much. This story illustrates the tremendous individual relativity of sensation. It is only relatively well developed: some are more and others less gifted at it. I would say that the extraverted sensation type would score highest in this field and would probably miss fewest points. The extraverted sensation type has the best photographic apparatus, as it were; he can quickly and objectively relate to outer facts. This is why this type is found among the good mountaineers, engineers and business people, all of whom have a wide and accurate awareness of outer reality in all its differentiations. This type will notice the texture of things—whether silk or wool. He will have a certain feeling for the material. Good taste is also generally present.

Jung says that such people very often give an impression of being rather soulless. Most people have met such a soulless engineer type, where you have the feeling that the man is absolutely dedicated to engines and their oils and sees everything from that angle. He produces no feeling and does not seem to think much either. Intuition is also completely lacking; that is for him just the realm of crazy fantasy. The extraverted sensation type calls everything approaching intuition 'mad fantasy,' completely idiotic imagination, something that has nothing to do with reality. He can even dislike thought, for if he is very one-sided he will consider that thinking is getting into the abstract instead of keeping to the facts. I had such an extraverted sensation type as a teacher in Natural Science, and we could never put a general theoretical question to him; he would call that getting off into abstract thinking and would say that we should stick to the facts—look at the worm and see what it looks like and then draw it, or look in the microscope and describe what you see there. That is Natural Science, and all the rest is fantasy and theory and nonsense. He was very good at explaining how factories make certain chemical products, and I still know the Haber Bosch process by heart. But when it came to the general theory of the inter-relation of elements, and so on, he did not teach us much. He said that was still uncertain in science and that it was theory which changed every year and was in constant evolution. So he skipped that side of the work.

Everything which might be a hunch or a guess, anything intuitive, appears to this type in an unpleasant form. If such a person had intuitions at all, they would be of a suspicious or grotesque nature. This professor once, in quite an amazing way, ventured into graphology. One day I brought him a letter written by my mother excusing me for not having been able to come to his class because I had had the flu. He looked at the writing and said: "Did your mother write that?" I said: "Yes." To which he only replied, "Poor child!" He only sensed the negative! He was like that. He would get suspicious fits about his *colleagues* and about the children in his class. You could see that he had some kind of dark intuition of something murky, for his intuition, being inferior, was like a dog sniffing in garbage pails. This inferior kind of intuition was very often right, but sometimes completely wrong! Sometimes he just had persecution ideas —dark suspicions without any foundation. A type who is so accurate on the factual level can suddenly get melancholy, suspicious premonitions, ideas of dark possibilities, and one does not know how these suddenly creep up. That is how inferior intuition came up in his case.

Normally, in the case of the extraverted sensation type, inferior intuition circles round the position of the subject, very often in dark feelings or hunches or premonitions about illnesses which he might get, or other misfortunes which might befall him. That means the inferior intuition is, in general, egocentric. Such a person often has a kind of negative, self-depreciative attitude. But if you get such people nicely drunk or very tired, or know them intimately so that they come out with their other side, they can produce the most amazing, weird, eerie ghost stories.

I knew a woman who was one of the best mountaineers in Switzerland. She was obviously an extraverted sensation type; only rational facts counted, and everything had its natural causes. She could climb all four thousand mountains not only in Switzerland but in the whole range of the Alps—the French, the Savoyan and the Austrian as well. But on dark evenings afterward, with a good fire burning, she would switch over and tell

*What an exhausted sensation
type intuits is. usually part
of his problem (inferiod
intuition).*

30   *Marie-Louise von Franz*

you the most eerie ghost stories, of the type you normally hear among the shepherds and peasants. It was quite wonderful to see this primitive fantasy coming out of her. The next morning when she put on her boots she would laugh it off and say it was all nonsense! What such a person intuits is usually an expression of his personal problem.

Another aspect of inferior intuition in an extraverted sensation type is a sudden attraction to Anthroposophy or some other cocktail of Eastern metaphysics, generally of a most otherworldly type. Very realistic engineers join such a movement with a completely uncritical mind and get quite lost in it. That is because their inferior intuition has such an archaic character. On their writing desks, amazingly enough, one will often find mystical texts, but of a rather second-class level. If asked why they read these books, they will say it is just nonsense but it helps them to go to sleep. Their superior function is still denying the inferior one. But if you ask the Anthroposophists at Dornach who supplied the money for their buildings, you will find that it came from just such extraverted sensation people. The American nation has a very great number of extraverted sensation types, and this is why such strange movements flourish especially well in the United States, to a much greater extent than in Switzerland. In Los Angeles you can find practically every kind of fantastic sect.

I remember once analyzing such a type. One day I had a telephone call from him. The man was sobbing at the telephone and said he was overwhelmed. "It happened—I cannot tell you, I am in danger!" Now this was not a hysterical person, and he did not have a latent psychosis or anything of the kind. You would never expect him to behave in this way. I was astonished and asked him if he would be able to go to the station and buy a ticket and come to Zürich (he was living in another town). He said he thought he could manage, so I told him to come. By the time he arrived he had snapped back into his superior sensation and brought me a basket of cherries—which we gaily ate together. I said: "And now what?" But he could not even tell me! In the meantime, by getting to the station and buying the cherries, he had got back into the upper level again. He had been attacked for a minute from the other level, and the only thing I got out of him was "For a minute I knew what God was! It is as if I realized God! And it shook me so much that I thought I would go mad, and now it is gone again. I remember it, but I cannot convey it any more, and I am no longer in it." There, via the inferior function, intuition, he suddenly had the whole collective unconscious and the Self. In a second—like a flash—it all came up and completely shook the upper part of his personality, but he could not hold it. That was the beginning of the coming up of inferior intuition, which shows its tremendously creative and positive, as well as its dangerous, aspect. Intuition has that quality of conveying a tremendous amount of meaningful content simultaneously. He saw the whole thing in one second; it came up for a minute, and then it went again. There he was munching cherries, back in his flat, ordinary, extraverted sensation world. That would be an example of the first genuine appearance of inferior intuition in such a type.

A great danger comes from the grip which the inferior function can get on a whole personality. I once knew an extraverted sensation type, a very efficient builder and good businessman, who had made a tremendous amount of money. He was very practical but built horrible houses. Only, the gadgets in them were perfect, so that people liked to live there even though from an artistic point of view the houses were awful. He was a good skier, dressed very well, admired women, and had the kind of refined sensuality which an extraverted sensation type can display. This man fell into the hands of an intuitive woman twenty years older than himself. She was a wild, fantastic mother figure and enormously fat. In her case this represented lack of discipline: introverted intuitive types are often terribly immoderate and exceed their reasonable limits both psychically and physically because of their inferior sensation. This woman lived only in her fantasies and was absolutely incapable of supporting herself financially. It was the typical union where the man provides the money and looks after the practical side of life, and the woman contributes the fantasy aspect.

I once went skiing with him. I was bored to tears! The only thing which he might have talked about in an interesting way was his business, but he did not talk of that to women, and otherwise he had nothing to say except that the sun was nice and the food not bad. To my great surprise, this man invited me to the Anthroposophs at Dornach to see a play. The *Goetheanum* was his "spiritual mother" and held a great attraction for him. He was absolutely gripped by the play, so moved that he was completely carried away. Afterward I was tactless enough to say that it was too high-up for me and that what I was longing for was a beefsteak! He was shocked out of his wits by my materialism. I was only about eighteen at the time and would be wiser now. But that was how his intuition worked. On the one side, it was projected into this woman, and on the other side there was Dornach. He tried to break with the woman, having realized the mother–son relationship, and hoped to park his inferior intuition in Dornach instead. This was certainly a step forward from just having it projected into a mother figure, for at least it was an attempt to assimilate it on an inner level. This is why my remark was so especially tactless. How the attempt worked out I have no idea, for I lost contact with him. But one should never make depreciative or hurtful remarks if people come out with their inferior function. It is terribly touchy.

Another example of inferior introverted intuition, but this time really inferior, illustrates the disgusting form and desperate abyss into which the inferior function can lead. Recently, in an American science fiction paper, I read the story of a man who invented an apparatus by which people could be dematerialized and re-materialized. He could, for instance, be here in Zürich and then suddenly materialize in New York. By means of such an apparatus it would be possible to dispense with airplanes and ships. First he experimented with ash trays and later with a fly. A few mistakes occurred at the beginning, but after the adjustment of several wires it seemed to work with the fly. In case anything went wrong, he wanted to be the first victim; so he put himself in the apparatus. Unfortunately, the experiment got stuck on the way, and he came out the other end with the head of an enormous fly! He tried to contact his wife, and covering up his head with a cloth so that she could not see it he told her she must try to free him and gave her various instructions. But nothing worked, and finally, in desperation, he asked her to kill him; out of kindness to him, she did. Afterward the story becomes one of the usual criminal types. When he is

a sensation type always wants to concretize his intuitions in some way

flys — are devilish insects (represent inferior intuition here)

dead and buried, the woman goes mad and gets put into an asylum. But then the first fly is found, the one which now has the man's head. The family, out of piety, has the fly put into a matchbox, which is sentimentally deposited on the tomb and an inscription states that the deceased was "a hero and a victim of science." I have spared you most of the disgusting and perverse details in the story which are expounded with great gusto.

There one sees how inferior intuition takes shape in a sensation production. Since the story is written by a sensation type, it gets disguised as completely practical sensation. The fly would represent inferior intuition which gets mixed up with the conscious personality. A fly is a devilish insect. In general, flies represent involuntary fantasies and thoughts which annoy one and buzz around in one's head and which one cannot chase away. Here, this scientist gets caught and victimized by an idea which involves murder and madness. In order to save the life of his wife, the family puts her into a lunatic asylum where she spends her time trying to catch flies, hoping to find the one which might be a part of her husband. At the end of the story the commissioner of police talks to the author and says that the woman was, after all, just mad. One sees that he would represent collective common sense—the verdict finally adopted by the writer, who admits that all this is just madness. If the writer had established the continuity of his inferior function, and had freed it from his extraverted sensation, then a really pure and clean story would have come out. In genuine fantasies, such as those of Edgar Allan Poe and the poet Gustav Meyrinck, intuition is established in its own right. These fantasies are highly symbolic and can be interpreted in a symbolic way. But a sensation type always wants to concretize his intuitions in some way.

The Introverted Sensation Type:
Inferior Extraverted Intuition

Many years ago, in the Psychological Club, we had a meeting at which members were asked to describe their type in their own

generally represent involuntary fantasies & thoughts which annoy one & buzz around in ones head —

words, instead of just quoting Jung's book on the types. Members were to describe how they experienced their own superior function. I have never forgotten an excellent paper that Mrs. Jung gave. It was only after hearing it that I felt I understood the introverted sensation type. In describing herself, she said that the introverted sensation type was like a highly sensitized photographic plate. When somebody comes into the room, such a type notices the way the person comes in, the hair, the expression on the face, the clothes, and the way the person walks. All this makes a very precise impression on the introverted sensation type; every detail is absorbed. The impression comes from the object to the subject. It is as though a stone fell into deep water: the impression falls deeper and deeper and sinks in. Outwardly, the introverted sensation type looks utterly stupid. He just sits and stares, and you do not know what is going on within him. He looks like a piece of wood with no reaction at all—unless he reacts with one of the auxiliary functions, thinking or feeling. But inwardly the impression is being absorbed.

The introverted sensation type, therefore, gives the impression of being very slow, which is not actually the case. It is only that the quick inner reactions go on underneath, and the outer reaction comes in a delayed way. These are the people who, if told a joke in the morning, will probably laugh at midnight. This type is very often misjudged and misunderstood by others because one does not realize what goes on within. If such a type can express his photographic impressions artistically, they can be reproduced either in painting or in writing. I have a strong suspicion that Thomas Mann was such an introverted sensation type. He describes every detail of a scene, and in his descriptions he gives the whole atmosphere of a room or a personality. This is a kind of sensitivity which takes in every smallest shade and detail.

The inferior intuition of this type is similar to that of the extraverted sensation type, for it also has a very weird, eerie, fantastic quality. But it is more concerned with the impersonal, collective outer world. With the builder I mentioned, for example, you can see that he is an extraverted sensation type. He picks up intuitions that concern himself. In his extraverted sensation, he is concerned with the collective outer world—with

THOMAS MANN — FELIX KRULL: CONFIDENCE MAN
— is material can be very prophetic — arch.
fantasies wh do not mainly represent
the problem of the dreamer but those of
his time — but 3 type gets stuck in concrete reality — but: possibilities do not exist.

road building or the building of big houses. But his intuition is
applied to himself; it is highly personal and mixed up with his
personal problems. With the introverted sensation type, the
movement comes from the object toward him. The novels by
Thomas Mann have a very subjective character. But the intuition of this type is concerned with events that go on in the
background; he picks up the possibilities and the future of the
outer surroundings.

I have seen in an introverted sensation type material which I
would call very prophetic—archetypal fantasies which do not
mainly represent the problem of the dreamer but those of his
time. The assimilation of these fantasies is very difficult because
sensation, the dominant function, is a function with which we
comprehend the here and now. The negative aspect of sensation is that the type gets stuck in concrete reality. As Jung once
noted, for them the future does not exist, future possibilities do
not exist, they are in the here and the now, and there is an iron
curtain before them. They behave in life as though it will always
be the same as it is now; they are incapable of conceiving that
things might change. The disadvantage of this type is that when
these tremendous inner fantasies well up, such a person has
great difficulty in assimilating them because of the accuracy and
slowness of his conscious function. If such a type is at all willing
to take his intuition seriously, he will be inclined to try to put it
down very accurately. But how can you do that? Intuition comes
like a flash, and if you try to put it down it has gone! So he does
not know how to deal with the problem and goes through
agonies, because the only way his inferior function can be
assimilated is by loosening the hold of the superior function.

I knew a woman, an introverted sensation type, who for many
years had very accurately painted the contents of her unconscious. It took her about three weeks to complete a painting.
The paintings were beautiful and worked out in every detail,
but, as I heard later, she did not paint the contents of her unconscious as they came; she corrected and improved the colors
and refined the details. She would say, "Naturally I improved
them aesthetically." Slowly the need to assimilate the inferior
function became imperative, and she was told that she should
speed up her painting and take the colors exactly as they were,

"They behave as though life will always be the same as it is now;
they are uncapabable of conceiving
that things might change."

however crude, and just put them on paper quickly. When I translated the contents of her dreams in this way, she got into a panic and said she could not, it was impossible. To have this put to her was like being knocked out, she could not do it, and she continued to paint in her usual way. Again and again she missed the coming up of the unconscious intuition, for she could not put it down as it came.

That is how the fight looks between the superior and inferior functions in the introverted sensation type. If you try to force him to assimilate intuition too quickly, he gets symptoms of giddiness or seasickness. He feels carried away from the solid ground of reality, and because he is so stuck there, he gets actual symptoms of seasickness. I knew one introverted sensation type woman who had to go to bed to do active imagination; otherwise she felt exactly as if she were on a boat.

Because the introverted sensation type's superior function is introverted, his intuition is extraverted and therefore is generally triggered off by outer events. Such a type might, while walking down a street, see a crystal in a shop window, and his intuition might suddenly grasp its symbolic meaning: the whole symbolic meaning of the crystal would flood into his soul. But that would have been triggered off by the outside event, since his inferior intuition is essentially extraverted. Naturally, he has the same bad characteristics as the extraverted sensation type; in both, intuitions are very often of a sinister character, and if not worked upon, therefore, the prophetic contents that break through will be pessimistic and negative.

Negative intuition sometimes does hit the target. It either hits the mark exactly, or it goes wildly astray. In general, when intuition is the main function and one of the other functions —either thinking or feeling—has been developed, the person can judge whether it might be the bull's eye or off in the woods, and therefore he holds back. But inferior intuition is primitive, and the sensation type either surprises you by hitting the bull's eye, which you can only admire, or else he comes up with hunches in which there is no truth—just pure invention!

In mythology intuition is very often represented by the Nose "I smell a rat!"

The Extraverted Intuitive Type: Inferior Introverted Sensation

Intuition is a function by which we conceive possibilities. A sensation type would call this object a bell, but a child would imagine all sorts of things you could do with it. It could be a church tower, this book could be a village, etc. In everything there is a possibility of development. In mythology, intuition is very often represented by the nose. One says: "I smell a rat"; that is, my intuition tells me that there is something wrong. I don't know quite what, but I can smell it! Then three weeks later the rat leaps out of its hole, and one says: "Oh, I smelt it, I had a hunch there was something in the air!" These are unborn possibilities, the germs of the future. Intuition is therefore the capacity for intuiting that which is not yet visible, future possibilities or potentialities in the background of a situation.

The extraverted intuitive type applies this to the outer world and therefore will score very high in surmising the future outer developments around him. Such types are very often found among business people. They are enterprisers who have the courage to manufacture and market new inventions. One finds them among journalists and frequently among publishers; they know what will be popular next year. They will bring out something which is not yet the fashion but soon will be, and they are the first to put it on the market. Stockbrokers, too, may have a certain knack which tells them that a particular stock will go up, that the market will be bullish or bearish, and they will make money through sensing the rise and fall of stocks. One finds them wherever there is something new brewing, even in the more spiritual realms. They will always be in the advance movement.

It is generally the creative artist who creates the future. A civilization which has no creative people is doomed. So the person who is really in touch with the future, with the germs of the future, is the creative personality. Now the extraverted intuitive, because he is capable of sniffing the wind and knowing what the

[handwritten annotation: Any kind of purposiveness poisons creative processes — Creative pco. are themselves introverted & so occupied to their creations they can not attend to bringing out their work.]

weather will be tomorrow, will see that this perhaps completely unknown painter or writer is the man of tomorrow, and therefore he will be fascinated. His intuition can recognize the value of such a creative person. Creative people themselves are introverted and are so occupied with their creations that they cannot attend to the bringing out of their work. The work itself takes up so much of their energy that they cannot be bothered with how it should be presented to the world, how to advertise it, or anything of that kind. Moreover, any kind of purposiveness poisons creative processes. Very often, then, the extraverted intuitive comes along and helps. But, naturally, if he does that all his life, he begins projecting a minor creative ability of his own on the artist, and so he loses himself. Sooner or later such people have to pull themselves out of their extraversion and say, "Now, even if it is on a minor scale, what is *my* creativeness?" And then they will be forced down into their inferior sensation, and instead of attending to other people's creativeness, they will have to attend to their own inferior sensation and to what might come out of it.

Intuition needs to look at things from afar or vaguely in order to function, so as to get a certain hunch from the unconscious, to half shut the eyes and not look at facts too closely. If one looks at things too precisely, the focus is on facts, and then the hunch cannot come through. That is why intuitives tend to be unpunctual and vague. A disadvantage of having this as a main function is that the intuitive type sows but rarely reaps. For instance, if one starts a new business, there are generally initial difficulties: the thing does not work immediately; it is necessary to wait a certain time for it to become profitable. The intuitive very often does not wait long enough. He starts the business, but that is enough for him; he sells out and loses on it, but the next owner makes a lot of money out of the same business. The intuitive is always the one who invents but who in the end gets nothing out of it. But if he is more balanced and can wait a little, and if he does not dissociate completely by identifying with his main function, then he is a person who can store up new things in all the corners of the world.

The extraverted intuitive tends not to attend to his body and his physical needs: he simply does not know when he is tired; he

does not notice it. It takes a breakdown to show him. He also
does not know when he is hungry. If he is an exaggerated one-
sided type, he does not know that he has any endosomatic feelings.

Inferior sensation, like all inferior functions, is in such people slow, heavy, and loaded with emotion. Because it is introverted, it is turned away from the outer world and its affairs. It
has, like all inferior functions, a mystical quality about it.

I once analyzed such an extraverted intuitive type, a businessman who had started a great many businesses in a foreign country and had also speculated a lot in gold mines and the like. He
always knew where possibilities were and made a large fortune
in a very short time, absolutely honestly—quite decently—
simply because he knew where to invest. He knew what was coming, what would happen in a few years, and he was always on the
spot first and got the whole business in hand. His introverted
sensation—he was rather a split personality—came up first as a
very dirty, bad-tempered tramp who appeared in his dreams.
The tramp sat around in inns, wore dirty clothes, and we did
not know what this fellow wanted of the dreamer. I induced him
to talk to the tramp in active imagination. The tramp said that
he had been responsible for the physical symptoms which had
brought the man to analysis, and that they had been sent
because he (the tramp) did not get enough attention. So, in active imagination, he asked what he should do. The tramp said
that he should, once a week, dress in clothes such as the tramp
wore, go for a walk in the country with him, and pay attention
to what he had to say.

I advised the dreamer to follow the advice precisely. The
result was that he took long walks through many parts of
Switzerland, staying in the most simple inns, unrecognized by
anybody. During this time he had a great number of overwhelming inner experiences which came through contact with nature:
the sunrise, and small things like seeing a certain flower in a corner of a rock, and so on. It struck right to the core of his personality and revealed a tremendous number of things. I can
only describe it as experiencing, in a very primitive way, the
Godhead in nature. He came back very silent and quieted, and
one had the feeling that something had moved in him which

"oh, the horse is a symbol of the
un — c !" — but extro: intuitive
(intro 'sensate) must attend to
"HORSE" even though he knows it
is a symbol"..

40   *Marie-Louise von Franz*

had never moved before. His compulsory symptoms disap-
peared completely during those weekly walks.

Then came the problem of how he could keep this experience
and avoid slipping back when he got home to his own country.
So we consulted the tramp again who said that he would let him
off the symptoms if he would take one afternoon each week, go
alone into nature, and continue his talks with him. The man
then left. From his letters I learnt that he did this for a while, but
then he slipped back to his old habits: there was too much work,
he was starting three new businesses, and there were so many
meetings. So he postponed the tramp, always saying, "Next
week, next week—sure I am coming, but next week." And then
he promptly got his symptoms back! That taught him; he
switched back and walked regularly and was all right again. It
then crystallized into buying a little farm and having a horse.
One afternoon a week he attended to his horse with what one
could only call religious devotion. The horse was his friend, so
to speak, and like a ritual he went to visit it and ride it and look
after it every week. From then on he had peace. I am sure a lot is
going on inwardly, but I haven't heard much from him except
for Christmas cards saying that he was getting on all right. And,
of course, photographs of the horse!

There one sees how the inferior function is the door to experiencing the deeper layers of the unconscious. This intuitive
type got out of his ego and ego purposes via this contact with
nature and with the horse. One sees very clearly that even if the
inferior function appears outside—in a horse, for example—it
obviously carries a symbolic meaning. Attending to the horse
was a first personification of the impersonal collective unconscious for him. It is important for an intuitive type to do this
concretely and very slowly, and not immediately exclaim: "Oh,
the horse is a symbol of the unconscious," etc. He must stick to
the actual horse and attend to it, even though he knows it is a
symbol.

Inferior sensation type has difficulties noticing needs of the body & controlling its appetites

The Introverted Intuitive Type:
Inferior Extraverted Sensation

The introverted intuitive type has the same capacity as the extraverted intuitive for smelling out the future, having the right guess or the right hunch about the not-yet-seen future possibilities of a situation. But his intuition is turned within, and therefore he is primarily the type of the religious prophet, of the seer. On a primitive level, he is the shaman who knows what the gods and the ghosts and the ancestral spirits are planning, and who conveys their messages to the tribe. In psychological language we should say that he knows about the slow processes which go on in the collective unconscious, the archetypal changes, and he communicates them to society. The prophets of the Old Testament, for instance, were people who, while the children of Israel were happily asleep—as the masses always are—from time to time told them what Yahweh's real intentions were, what he was doing now, and what he wanted his people to do. The people generally did not enjoy hearing these messages.

Many introverted intuitives are to be found among artists and poets. They generally are artists who produce very archetypal and fantastic material, such as you find in Nietzsche's *Thus Spoke Zarathustra* or in Gustav Meyrinck's *The Golem* and Kubin's *The Other Side.* This kind of visionary art is generally only understood by later generations, as a representation of what was going on in the collective unconscious at that time.

The inferior sensation of this type also has difficulties in noticing the needs of the body and controlling its appetites. Swedenborg had a vision in which God himself told him he should not eat so much! He ate naturally, without the slightest self-discipline and with complete unawareness. Swedenborg was a typical introverted intuitive, the prophet or seer type, and he was simply coarse and uninhibited about over-eating. The introverted intuitive also suffers, as the extraverted intuitive does, from a tremendous vagueness where facts are concerned.

As an illustration of the more ridiculous aspect of the inferior sensation of an introverted intuitive, I offer the following story. An introverted intuitive woman was present when I gave a lecture on early Greek philosophy and was terribly moved and impressed by it. Afterward, she asked me to give her private lessons on the subject of pre-Socratic philosophy, as she wanted to get deeper into this field. She invited me to tea and, as happens very often when you have to give lessons to introverted intuitives, she wasted the first hour in telling me how moved she was and what she conceived to be at the back of my mind and what she believed we could do together, and so on. The second hour also got wasted in the same way, and, as I felt I should earn my money and get her going somehow, I insisted we look at a book which I had brought and proceed in a systematic way. She agreed, but added that I must leave her alone: she had to do it quite her own way. I noticed that she was getting nervous.

When I came for the next hour, she said she had found the best way to get into the problem: namely, that she could naturally not study Greek philosophy without knowing about the Greeks, and she could not know about the Greeks before knowing quite concretely about their country. So she had started to draw a map of Greece, and she showed me the map. It had taken a lot of time. With her inferior sensation she had first had to buy paper and pencils and ink. That excited her enormously; she was absolutely in heaven about her achievement! She said that she could not yet go on with philosophy; she had first to finish the map. So by the next time she had colored it! That went on for a few months, and then her intuition picked another theme, and we never got down to Greek philosophy. She left Zürich and I did not see her again until about fifteen years later; then she told me a long story of how she was still impressed and moved by the lessons on Greek philosophy which I had given her and all that she had gained from them. She had just drawn a map. She was a very extreme case of introverted intuition. But I must admit, in looking back, that I see what a really numinous thing it was for that woman to draw this map of Greece; for the first time she had got in touch with her inferior sensation.

The introverted intuitive is often so completely unaware of outer facts that his reports have to be treated with the greatest

Nose - IT does not notice what is right under his NOSE.

Inferior sensation of IN is extremely intense but breaks thru only here & there & then fades away from field of awareness

The Four Irrational Types   43

care. Though he does not lie consciously, he can tell the most appalling untruths, simply because he does not notice what is right under his nose. I very often distrust ghost reports, for instance, and reports about para-psychological facts for those reasons. Introverted intuitives are very much interested in such fields, but because of their weakness in observing facts and their lack of concentration on the external situation, they can tell you the most appalling nonsense and swear it is true. They pass by an absolutely amazing number of outer facts and just do not take them in. I remember, for instance, driving with an introverted intuitive type one autumn, and in the fields the potatoes were being dug up and there were bonfires. I had noticed that for quite some time and was enjoying the sight. Suddenly the driver stopped the car in horror, sniffed, and said, "Something is burning! Is it coming from outside?" We looked at the brakes, and everything was all right; then we decided it was outside after all. It was the bonfires! The bonfires were everywhere, and to me it was obvious that the smell of burning came from them. But an introverted intuitive can drive for an hour through the country with such phenomena all about and not notice a thing. And then *suddenly* he will be struck by the fact and make completely incorrect deductions. His inferior sensation has the quality which all inferior functions have, namely, that it comes up into consciousness in islands; sometimes it functions, and then it disappears. Suddenly a smell is intensely realized, whereas three-quarters of an hour before it was not realized at all, but then suddenly it is taken in with great intensity.

The inferior sensation of an introverted intuitive is extremely intense, but it breaks through only here and there and then fades again from the field of awareness. The introverted intuitive has particular trouble in approaching sex because it involves his inferior extraverted sensation. It is most tragically mirrored in the works of Nietzsche, for instance, where, toward the end of his career, shortly before he went insane, very coarse sexual allusions penetrate his poems and also appear in *Thus Spoke Zarathustra*. When he went insane, he apparently produced material of that kind, which was destroyed after his death because of its absolutely distasteful character. Inferior extraverted sensation in his case was very much connected with

Jakob Boehme — his actual vision was set in motion by seeing a ray of light striking a tin plate — An outer SENSATION FACT started off the process of individuation in him

women and sex, in a completely concrete way, and he didn't know how to deal with the problem at all.

The positive aspect of inferior extraverted sensation in the case of an introverted intuitive is to be found in an interesting way in the illumination experience of Jakob Boehme, a German mystic and an introverted intuitive type. He had a wife and six children for whom he never earned any money. He was in constant trouble with them because his wife always said that instead of writing books about God and fantasizing about the inner development of the Godhead he would do better to see that his family had something to eat. He was absolutely crucified between these two poles of life. Now his greatest inner experience, a revelation of the Godhead upon which all his later writings are based, came from seeing a ray of light being reflected in a tin plate. That sensation experience snapped him into an inner ecstasy, and within a minute he saw, so to speak, the whole mystery of the Godhead. For years he did nothing except slowly translate into discursive language what he had seen inwardly in one minute, in one second! His writing is so emotional and chaotic because he tried to describe this one experience in so many amplifications. But the actual vision was set in motion by seeing a ray of light striking a tin plate on his table. This implies extraverted sensation: an outer sensation fact started off the process of individuation in him. Here one can see, besides the inferior aspect of extraverted sensation, this strange character of wholeness, the mystical aspect, which the inferior function often has. It is interesting that even Swedenborg's over-eating connected him with the Godhead. His inferior sensation was connected with his deepest and greatest concern.

(A period of questions and answers follows.)

Question: I would like to ask whether the ecstatic state is usually connected with the inferior function.

Dr. von Franz: Yes, it is connected in that it is normally started off by an experience of the inferior function.

Question: Would you say that the intuitive types tend to be more sensitive to what we call subliminal stimuli?

Dr. von Franz: Yes, in general I would say that both intuitive types are. They have to be, for they have to keep their consciousness constantly unfocused and dim in order to get those hunches. They are sensitive to the atmosphere of a place. Probably intuition is a kind of sense perception via the unconscious or a sort of subliminal sense perception. It is a way of operating through subliminal sense perception instead of through conscious perception.

Question: Both the extraverted intuitive and Jakob Boehme seem to have distinctly introverted sensation. Shouldn't the introverted intuitive have a more extraverted sensation?

Dr. von Franz: Yes, but Boehme had! My "horse man" (to describe him briefly) realized inner depth and became silent through his experience; he hasn't even told me much about it. He has only made allusions that something deep was going on. Boehme, on the other hand, exteriorized his insight—constructed a system of outer reality, of God and of evil in the world. He made a whole philosophy of it, but turned outward, while personally he was very introverted. He was a shy little shoemaker.

Something else very interesting about Boehme is that as long as he was crucified between his nagging wife, who said he had better make good shoes and feed his six children, and speculating about a Godhead, he was very productive. But after his first book was published, a German baron felt so sorry for him, and felt so strongly that he was a great seer, that he took all his outer troubles away by paying for his family's support. From then on Boehme's writing gets full of resentment and repetitions. It sterilized his creativeness. As you know, on his tomb is an image of the Godhead like this:) (. This is really tragic, as it shows that he could not unite the light and the dark sides; that remained an insoluble problem to him. In my experience, this is connected with the very simple fact that he accepted money from this baron and by that escaped the torture of his inferior function.

By accepting money from the Baron Boehme, escaped [judgment] of his inferior [func]. e Boehme became little ether [of his] writings became full of repetitions.

46   *Marie-Louise von Franz*

To be crucified between the superior and the inferior functions is vitally important. I can only warn you that if you ever feel like saving such artists or prophets, for God's sake look at the case first very circumspectly and see how much you can afford to help them. If you buy them off reality, then they lose all sense of it. You have not helped them in the least. This type *will* beg you to help them out of their trouble; on their knees they will beg you to save them from the torture of outer reality with which they can't cope. But if you "save" them, the creative core of their personality is destroyed. That does not mean that if they are starving you cannot give them something to survive, or give them help from time to time when the situation is bad, but don't let them off the problem of reality because, strangely enough, that sterilizes the inner process as well. That happened to Boehme, and because of it he was not able to unite the opposites, neither in his system nor in his life. What Baron von Merz did was really to destroy him by unwise charity.

the emphasis will always be on the object, not the idea

CHAPTER III
The Four Rational Types

The Extraverted Thinking Type:
Inferior Introverted Feeling

This type is to be found among organizers, people in high office and government positions, in business, in law and among scientists. They can compile useful encyclopedias. They dig up all the dust in old libraries and do away with the inhibiting factors in science which are caused by clumsiness or laziness or a lack of clarity in language. The extraverted thinking type establishes order by taking a definite stand and saying, "If we say so-and-so, we mean so-and-so." They put clarifying order into the outer situation. At a business meeting, such a man will say that one should get at the basic facts and then see how to proceed. A lawyer who has to listen to all the chaotic reports of contending parties is able, with his superior thinking function, to see which are the real conflicts and which the pseudo-contentions, and then to arrange a solution satisfactory to all parties. The emphasis will always be upon the object, not on the idea. Such a

If you look for un-e motivations of E T they will consist of childlike naive belief in peace, charity & justice

In solitude such a person would have to ask himself whether his work

lawyer will not fight for the *idea* of democracy or domestic peace; his whole mind will be absorbed with and swallowed up by the outer objective situation.

If one were to ask him about his subjective attitude or ideas on a certain subject, he would be at a loss, for he is not concerned with that area of life and would be completely unconscious of any personal motive. Generally, if you search for the unconscious motivations, they will consist in a childlike naive belief in peace, charity and justice. If pressed into saying what he understood by "justice," he would be quite bewildered and probably throw you out of his office because he was "too busy." The subjective element remains in the background of his personality. The premises of his high ideals remain within the realm of his inferior feeling function. He will have a mystical feeling attachment to his ideals, but one would have to drive him into a corner to find out about them. Feeling attachments to certain ideals or to people are present, but they never appear in daytime activities. Such a man might spend his whole life settling problems, re-organizing firms, and stating things clearly; only at the end of his life would he start to ask himself mournfully what he had really lived for. At such a moment he would fall into his inferior function.

I once talked to a man of this type who was terribly overworked and needed a long holiday. He gave *me* a lot of good advice, saying *I* should go on a holiday, and when I asked him why *he* didn't, he replied: "My God, I should be alone too much and get much too melancholy!" In solitude, such a person will ask himself whether his work is really important. He will remember how he saved someone from being robbed and so on, but has he improved the world? Such feelings would have come up in this gentleman, and he would have felt like falling into an abyss. He would have had to recheck his whole evaluation of things. Naturally, therefore, he avoided taking any holidays—until he fell and broke his hip and had to stay in bed six months. That is how nature imposes the inferior function on such people!

The extraverted thinking type has, as I said already, a kind of mystical feeling attachment for ideals and often also for people. But this deep, strong, warm feeling hardly ever comes out. I remember an extraverted thinking type who, when he once

is really important ... until he fell & broke his hip & had to stay in bed for 6 mo. That is how the inferior function is imposed by nature on such peo-

came out with his feeling for his wife, really moved me. But when I talked to his wife it was deplorable to see how little she knew of it, because, as a mad extravert, he would spend the whole day in his profession, milling around in life, and those deep feelings were never expressed. If his wife had been dying of consumption he would not have noticed it until he was at the funeral. And *she* did not realize the depth of his feeling for her and that, in a deep sense, he was loyal and faithful to her; that was hidden and not expressed in his life. It remained introverted and did not move toward the object. It took quite a few sessions to get a better understanding in the marriage and to make the wife realize that her husband really loved her. He was so terribly occupied with the outer world, and his feeling was so hidden and unexpressed in his life, that his wife did not realize what a tremendous hidden role these feelings played within him.

Introverted feeling, even if it is the main function, is very difficult to understand. A very good example of it is the Austrian poet Rainer Maria Rilke. He once wrote: "*Ich liebe dich, was geht's dich an.*" ("I love you, but it's none of your business.") That is love for love's sake! Feeling is very strong, but it does not flow toward the object. It is rather like being in a state of love with oneself. Naturally, this kind of feeling is very much misunderstood, and such people are considered very cold. But they are not at all; the feeling is all within them. On the other hand, they have a very strong hidden influence on the surrounding society, for they have secret ways of establishing values. For example, such a feeling type may never express his feeling but simply behave as though he thought one thing was valuable and another not: this exerts a certain impact on other people. When the feeling is inferior, it is even more hidden and more absolute. The lawyer I described had his idea of justice, and this would have very suggestive effects on other people; that is, his hidden feeling for justice would unconsciously influence other people in the same direction without his ever noticing it. It would really dictate not only his own fate but also that of others, though invisibly.

The hidden, introverted feeling of the extraverted thinking type establishes strong invisible loyalties. Such people are among the most faithful of all friends, even though they may only write at Christmas. They are absolutely faithful in their feeling, but one has to move toward it to get to know of its existence.

Outwardly, the extraverted thinking type does not give the impression of having strong feeling. In a politician, the inferior feeling function might unconsciously manifest itself in a deep-rooted and steadfast loyalty to his country. But it might also induce him to drop an atom bomb or commit some other destructive act. Unconscious and undeveloped feeling is barbaric and absolute, and therefore sometimes hidden destructive fanaticism suddenly bursts out of the extraverted thinking type. These people are incapable of seeing that, from a feeling standard, other people might have another value, for they do not question the inner values which they defend. Where they definitely feel that something is right, they are incapable of showing their feeling standpoint, but they never doubt their own inner values.

These hidden introverted feelings of the extraverted thinking type are sometimes very childish. After the death of such people, one sometimes finds notebooks in which childish poems have been written to a faraway woman whom they never met in their lives, and in which a lot of sentimental, mystical feeling is poured out. They often ask to have these poems destroyed after death. The feeling is hidden; it is, in a way, the most valuable possession they have, but all the same it is sometimes strikingly infantile. Sometimes the feeling remains entirely with the mother and never comes out of the childhood realm; one may then find touching documents about the attachment to her.

Another way in which infantile feeling can manifest itself in extraverted thinking types is instanced in the case of Voltaire, the French philosopher. He, as you know, fought the Catholic Church with all his might. He was the author of the famous slogan *Ecrasez l'infâme.* He was an intellectual and a typical representative of the age of enlightenment. On his deathbed, however, he got jittery, asked for *extreme unction* and took it with a great upwelling of pious feeling. There he showed, at the end of his life, that he was completely split: his mind had left an original religious experience, but his feeling had stayed there.

When it came to death—which one has to meet as a whole person—his feeling came up and overwhelmed him in a completely undifferentiated way. All sudden conversions have this quality: they are due to the sudden eruption of the inferior function.

The Introverted Thinking Type:
Inferior Extraverted Feeling

The main activity of this type is not so much trying to establish order in outer objects; it is more concerned with ideas. Someone who would say that one should not start with facts, but first clarify one's ideas, would belong to the introverted thinking type. His wish to bring order into life starts off with the idea that, if one is muddle-headed from the very start, one will never get anywhere. It is first necessary to know what ideas to follow and where they come from; one must clean up muddle-headedness by digging into the background of one's thoughts. All philosophy is concerned with the logical processes of the human mind, with the building up of ideas. This is the realm where introverted thinking is mostly at work. In science these are the people who are perpetually trying to prevent their colleagues from getting lost in experiments and who, from time to time, try to get back to basic concepts and ask what we are really doing mentally. In physics, there is generally one professor for practical physics and another for theoretical physics: one lectures on the Wilson Chamber and the building up of experiments, the other on mathematical principles and the theory of science. In all the various sciences there are always those who try to clean out the basic theories of their scientific realm. The extraverted historian of art will try to find out about the facts and try to prove, for instance, that a certain type of Madonna was painted earlier or later than another type, and he will try to connect that with the history and background of the artist. The introvert might ask what right one had to judge a work of art? He would say that first we should understand what we mean by art; otherwise we shall get into a muddle. The introverted thinking type always goes back to the subjective idea, namely, to what the subject is doing in the whole matter.

The feeling of the introverted thinking type is extraverted. He has the same kind of strong, loyal and warm feeling described as typical for the extraverted thinking type, but with the difference that the feeling of the introverted thinking type flows toward definite objects. While the extraverted thinking type deeply loves his wife but says with Rilke, "I love you, but it is none of your business," the feeling of the introverted thinking type is tied to external objects. He would therefore say, in the Rilke style, "I love you, and it will be your business; I'll make it your business!" Otherwise, the introverted thinking type's feeling has very much the same characteristics as the inferior feeling of the extraverted thinking type—very black and white judgments, either yes or no, love or hate. His feeling can be very easily poisoned by other people and by the collective atmosphere. The inferior feeling of both types is sticky, and the extraverted thinking type has that kind of invisible faithfulness which can last endlessly. The same is true for the extraverted feeling of the introverted thinking type, except that it will not be invisible. If you evaluate it positively, it will be faithful; but in a negative evaluation, it is sticky. It resembles the glue-like flow of feeling in an epileptoid person; it has the kind of sticky, doglike attachment which, especially to the beloved, is not always amusing. You could compare the inferior feeling of an introverted thinking type to the flow of hot lava from a volcano: it only moves about five meters an hour, but it devastates everything in its way. But it also has all the advantages of a primitive function, for it is tremendously genuine and warm. When an introverted thinking type loves, there is no calculation in it. It will be totally for the sake of the other, but it will be primitive. The inferior feeling of this type is about as if a lioness would like to play with a baby. It has no other intention than to play, but it rubs itself, purring, against his leg, or eats him up, or gives him a great blow so that he falls over, and then it licks his face. But there is no calculation in it; it is just an expression of feeling, just as a dog wags his tail! What touches people in the feeling of domestic animals is just this lack of calculation.

In both thinking types inferior feeling is without calculation, whereas people who have differentiated feeling are, in a hidden way, calculating. They always put a little bit of ego into it. I once met the boss of a typist and wondered how she stood such a horror for a single day! But she was a feeling type. She only smiled and said that he was her boss so she made the best of it; by looking at him closely, she could find that he had this and that positive quality. One could say that to see good possibilities and recognize them is admirable, but on the other hand there is a little calculation in it: she wanted to keep her place with her boss, so she made that positive feeling effort. That would never happen to the inferior feeling of a thinking type! I could never have stood it: I would rather not eat. Such is the great difference between inferior and differentiated feeling. The feeling type had found a few positive qualities in that horrible man and put up with him. She did not deny all the negative things I saw in him, but she said he never worked overtime, and he gave merit to those who worked for him. She discovered a few positive factors in him and stayed there.

In *Psychological Types,* Jung explains some of the misunderstandings between the types. If I had said that this office girl was calculating and acting out of opportunism, it would have been absolutely wrong; that was only a background motive in her case. Such a judgment would be the negative projection of the opposite type. It is not that she is just an opportunist or is acting in a calculating way in having such positive feelings; she has differentiated feeling. She therefore never has strong feeling reactions; she knows that where there is value there is always something negative. Nothing is quite black or absolutely white, but everything is grayish in reality. She has that kind of philosophical attitude. I saw the calculation and opportunism because the introverted thinking type generally sees the negative side and will say that the feeling type always knows on which side his bread is buttered. On the other hand, one can say that inferior feeling has the advantage that there is really no calculation in it. The ego has nothing to do with it. But naturally this can create unadapted situations. Think, for instance, of *The Blue Angel,* where a professor falls for a vamp in a cabaret and faithfully and loyally gets ruined by her. That would be the

tragedy of the inferior feeling function. One could honor him
for his faithfulness, but one could just as well say that he was a
fool and that his inferior feeling had very bad taste. The inferior feeling of a thinking type shows either very good or very
bad taste. A thinking type can sometimes choose very valuable
people for his friends, or he can pick absolutely the wrong ones;
the inferior function has both aspects, and it rarely fits into conventional patterns.

The Extraverted Feeling Type:
Inferior Introverted Thinking

The extraverted feeling type is characterized by the fact that his
main adaptation is carried by an adequate evaluation of outer
objects and an appropriate relation to them. This type will
therefore make friends very easily, will have very few illusions
about people, but will be capable of evaluating their positive
and negative sides appropriately. These are well adjusted, very
reasonable people who roll along amiably through society, can
get what they want quite easily, and can somehow arrange it that
everybody is willing to give them what they want. They lubricate
their surroundings so marvelously that life goes along very easily. You find them frequently among women, and they generally
have a very happy family life with a lot of friends. Only if they
are in some way neurotically dissociated do they become a bit
theatrical and a little mechanical and calculating. If one goes to
a luncheon party with an extraverted feeling type, she (or he) is
capable of saying little things like "What a nice day it is today, I
am so glad to see you again, I haven't seen you for a long time!"
And they really mean it! With that the car is lubricated, and the
party goes. One feels happy and warmed up. They spread a kind
of atmosphere of acceptance, and it is agreeable: "We appreciate each other, so we are going to have a good day together."
They make those in their surroundings feel wonderful, and in
the midst of that they swim along happily and create a pleasant

social atmosphere. Only if they overdo it, or if their extraverted feeling is already worn out and they therefore should start to think, do you notice that this becomes a bit of a habit, that it becomes a phrase which they say mechanically. For instance, I once noticed an extraverted feeling type, on a dreadful day when there was a horrible fog outside, saying mechanically: "Isn't it a wonderful day!" I thought, "Oh dear, your main function is rattling!"

Because people of the extraverted feeling type have such a tremendous capacity for objectively feeling the other person's situation, they are usually the ones who most genuinely sacrifice themselves for others. If one is alone at home with the flu, it is certainly an extraverted feeling type who will turn up first and ask who is doing the shopping and how he can help. Other types are not so quick and practical about feeling their way into a situation. To the others, even though their affection might run as deeply, it would not occur that they could do this or that to help, either because they are introverts or because another function is dominant in their system. So you find the extraverted feeling type always jumping into the breach, for wherever something does not function properly he realizes it at once. He sees the importance or the value of what should be done, and he just does it. Naturally, this can lead to resistance against the outer situation.

In general, this type has very good taste in the choice of partners and friends, but he is a little conventional about it. He wouldn't risk choosing someone too much out of the ordinary; he wants to remain in a socially acceptable framework. The extraverted feeling type dislikes thinking, because that is his inferior function, and what he dislikes most of all is introverted thinking—thinking about philosophical principles or abstractions or basic questions of life. Such deeper questions are carefully avoided, and there is the reaction that thinking about such problems is melancholy. The unfortunate thing is that he does think of such things, but is not aware of it, and because his thinking is neglected, it tends to become negative and coarse. It consists of coarse, primitive thinking judgments, without the slightest differentiation and very often with a negative tinge. I

have also seen in the extraverted feeling type very negative
thoughts about the neighboring people, very critical—I would
say over-critical—thinking judgments, which he never allows
really to come out. Jung says that the extraverted feeling type can
sometimes be the coldest person on earth. It may happen that, if
you get lured into this well-lubricated car of his extraverted feeling and feel "we like each other and get along well together,"
suddenly one day he will say something to you which will feel
like getting smacked on the head with a block of ice! One cannot guess what cynical, negative thoughts he might have. He is
not aware of them, but they pop out when he begins to have the
'flu' or when he is rushed—in such moments when the inferior
function wells up and the control of the superior function fails.

An extraverted feeling type once dreamt that she should
establish a bird observation station. She saw in the dream a ce-
ment building, a tower built high up in the air, and on the top
was a kind of laboratory where one observed birds. We have
such a *Vogelbeobachtungsstation* (Bird Observatory) at Sempach
where rings are put on birds to know how long they live, and
where they go, and so on; she was to do that. So we thought she
should try to be aware of autonomous thoughts which would, as
it were, alight on her head and go again. That is how thoughts
operate in a feeling type; he has bird-thoughts alighting on his
head and flying off again. Before he can say, "What am I thinking?" the thought is gone again. This woman agreed, and I
asked her how it could be done technically. She said she would
take a little notebook and a pencil and carry them around with
her, and when she had a sudden thought she would just jot it
down. We would see afterward how they were connected. Next
time she brought one piece of paper, and on it was "If my son-
in-law died, my daughter would come back home." She got such
a shock from that thought that she never put a ring on a second
bird! That one bird was quite enough for a long time. She then
confessed something even more interesting: she said that in a
way she knew she sometimes had such thoughts but always
figured that if she didn't write them down they would not be effective. If she did, they would act like black magic and affect her
surroundings. So, she avoided looking at them.

Now that is exactly wrong. It is just the other way round: if the feeling type is aware of his negative thoughts, they don't act like black magic. They are depotentiated of any destructive effect. It is just when they are left alone and fly around his head without being caught that they actually have a destructive influence on his surroundings. If one analyzes an extraverted feeling type and is somewhat sensitive to the atmosphere, one very often gets a bit frozen or cooled down in spite of his amiability. One can sense these negative thoughts swarming around in his head. Such thoughts hit one in a disagreeable way. One sometimes sees a kind of cold flash in the eyes and knows that there is a very negative thought about, but the next minute it is gone. It gives one the creeps. Such thoughts are generally based on a very cynical outlook on life: the dark side of life which is illness and death and other such things. A kind of second philosophy of life, cynical and negativistic, creeps around in the background. In the extraverted feeling type, these thoughts are introverted, and therefore they are very often turned against the subject himself. At bottom he allows himself to think that he is a nobody, that his life is worthless, and that everybody else might develop and get on the path of individuation, but he is hopeless. These thoughts dwell in the back of his mind. From time to time, when he is depressed, or not well off, or especially when he introverts (that is when he is alone for half a minute), this negative thing whispers at the back of his head: "You are nothing, everything about you is wrong." These thoughts are coarse and primitive and very undifferentiated; they are generalized judgments and are like a cold draught which blows through the room and makes you shiver. The effect is that the extraverted feeling type naturally hates to be alone when such negative thoughts could come up, so as soon as he has realized one or two of them he quickly switches on the radio or rushes out to meet other people. He never has time to think! But he carefully arranges his life in that way.

If this woman who had the one little thought *("My only daughter would come back home!")* had dug deeper, she would have had to say to herself, "Okay, let's face that thought! What am I after? If I have such a thought what is the premise, and what is the conclusion to be drawn?" She could then have developed the following thought: the premise is something like a devouring mother's attitude, and the conclusion is that she wants the son-in-law removed. Why? For what purpose? She could, for example, have said, "Assuming that my daughter does come home, what then?" And then she would have seen how unpleasant it would actually be to have a sour old maid of a daughter at home. In continuing the thought, she would have probably dropped into a deeper layer and said, "And what then? If my children have now left home, what is the real purpose of my life?" She would have had to philosophize about the future purpose of her life: "Has life still a meaning once one has brought up the children and started them into life? And, if so, what is it? What is the meaning of life altogether?" She would have been confronted with the deep, but generally human, philosophical questions which she had never faced before, and that would have brought her into deep water. She naturally could not have solved the problem, but she might have had a dream to help the whole process along. With her inferior thinking function she would have started on a quest for the meaning of life. Because she was an extraverted feeling type, the quest would have been a completely introverted, inner thing, like developing an introverted philosophical view of life. That would have needed being alone, being alone a long time in her room and slowly getting aware of the dark underground of her thoughts.

The easy escape, which I have seen in several cases of extraverted feeling types, is that they get out of the difficulty by simply selling their souls to some already established system. One case, I remember, got converted to Catholicism and simply took over scholastic philosophy; from then on she quoted only scholastic authors. That was, in a way, taking up the thinking function, but taking it up in an already established form. The same thing can be done with Jungian psychology: it will become a matter of simply repeating the concepts by heart in a mechanical way, but never working out one's own standpoint. It is a kind of pupil-like, uncreative attitude which just takes over the entire system unchecked and never asks, "What do *I* think about it? Does this really convince me? Does it coincide with the facts I have checked?" If such people then meet others who themselves know how to think, they get fanatical because they feel helpless. They fight for the system they have chosen with a certain apostle-like fanaticism because they feel uncertain about the basis of the thinking system: how the system developed, its basic concepts, etc. They are uncertain about it and have the feeling that it could be thrown over by a good thinker, so they adopt an aggressive attitude.

Another danger is that if an extraverted feeling type once starts to think he gets completely caught up in it. Either he cannot cut off his relationships sufficiently to be alone and think, or, if he succeeds—which is already great progress—in cutting off these outer ties, he gets terribly caught by them and loses sight of life. He disappears into books, or into a library, where he gets covered with dust and is no longer able to switch to any other activity. He gets swallowed by his task. Both developments are very well represented in Goethe's *Faust* where, first, there is the scientist absolutely cut off from life in the dusty study, and then, when Faust frees himself and goes out into life, the inferior thinking of the feeling type is represented by Wagner, the pupil-like servant who just repeats the banal phrases he has picked up in books. A famous example of the inferior thinking of an extraverted feeling type is Goethe's *Conversations with Eckermann*. It is an amazing collection of platitudes. There you see the Wagner side of Goethe very visibly exposed to the world. He has also published a collection of maxims which you might meet on the back leaf of every calendar! They are very true, you can rarely object to them in any way, but they are so banal that any sheep could have thought of them. That is Wagner at work in the great poet.

The Introverted Feeling Type: Inferior Extraverted Thinking

The introverted feeling type also has the characteristic that he adapts to life mainly by feeling, but in an introverted way. This type is very difficult to understand. Jung says in *Psychological Types* that the saying "still waters run deep" applies to this type. They have a highly differentiated scale of values, but they do not express them outwardly; they are affected by them within. One often finds the introverted feeling type in the background where important and valuable events are taking place, as if their introverted feeling had told them "that is the real thing." With a kind of silent loyalty, and without any explanation, they turn up in places where important and valuable inner facts, archetypal constellations, are to be found. They also generally exert a positive secret influence on their surroundings by setting standards. The others observe them, and though they say nothing, for they are too introverted to express themselves much, they set certain standards. Introverted feeling types, for instance, very often form the ethical backbone of a group: without irritating the others by preaching moral or ethical precepts, they themselves have such correct standards of ethical values that they secretly emanate a positive influence on those around them. One has to behave correctly because they have the right kind of value standard, which always suggestively forces one to be decent if they are present. Their differentiated introverted feeling sees what is inwardly the really important factor.

The thinking of this type is extraverted. In striking contrast to their silent and inconspicuous outer appearance, persons of the introverted feeling type are generally interested in an immense number of outer facts. In their conscious personality they do not move about much; they tend to sit in their badger's hole. But their extraverted thinking roams about in an extraordinary range of outer facts. If they want to use their extraverted thinking in a creative way, they have the usual extravert's difficulty of being overwhelmed by too much material, too many references and too many facts, so their inferior extraverted thinking sometimes just gets lost in a morass of details through which they can no longer find their way. The inferiority of their extraverted thinking very often expresses itself in a certain monomania: they have actually only one or two thoughts with which they race through a tremendous amount of material. Jung always characterized the Freudian system as a typical example of extraverted thinking.

Freud = INFJ ?

Jung never said anything about Freud's type as a human being; he only pointed out in his books that Freud's *system* represents extraverted thinking. What I add now is my own personal
conviction, namely, that Freud himself was an introverted feeling type, and therefore his writings bear the characteristics of
his inferior extraverted thinking. In all his works the basic ideas
are few. With them he has raced through an enormous amount
of material, and the whole system is completely oriented toward
the outer object. If one reads biographical notes about Freud,
one sees that as a person he had a most differentiated way of
treating other people. He was an excellent analyst. He had also
a kind of hidden "gentlemanliness" which had a positive
influence upon his patients and upon his surroundings. One
must really in his case make a distinction between his theory
and his personality as a human being. I think, from what one
hears about him, that he belonged to the introverted feeling
type.

The advantage of inferior extraverted thinking is what I just
now characterized negatively as "racing with a few ideas
through a tremendous amount of material." (Freud himself
complained that his dream interpretations felt awfully
monotonous; the same interpretation of every dream was boring even to him.) If this tendency is not overdone, and if the introverted feeling type is aware of the danger of his inferior
function and keeps a check on it, it has the great advantage of
being simple, clear and intelligible. But this is not enough, and
the introverted feeling type is obliged to drill a bit deeper and
try to specify and differentiate his extraverted thinking. Otherwise he will fall into the trap of intellectual monomania.
Therefore, he has to specify his thinking; that is, he should
make the hypothesis that each fact he quotes in proof of his
ideas illustrates them in a slightly different way, and with this
point in view, his ideas should be reformulated each time. In
that way he maintains the living process of contact between
thought and fact, instead of simply imposing his thought upon
facts. Inferior extraverted thinking has just the same negative
tendencies of becoming tyrannical, stiff and unyielding, and in
that way not quite adapted to its object, that all other inferior
functions have.

(A period of questions and answers follows.)

Question: Are the types—the attitudinal and function types—equally distributed? Are there as many extraverts as introverts?

Dr. von Franz: We don't know for the whole of mankind; we have no studies of Chinese villages and such places. In general, we often speak of different nations as types; we say, for example, that the Swiss are, on the whole, introverted sensation types. This would imply that in certain groups one type sometimes prevails. Although there are many Swiss who are another type, there is a statistically dominant prevalence of the introverted sensation type. You can observe it, for instance, in the high standard in Swiss crafts: the watch-making industry needs an *introverted* attitude with differentiated sensation to operate correctly. So in the different countries and nations you could say that one type is dominant and creates a prevalent attitude in groups. But when you sum it all up—whether there are as many of each type—I do not know. It would need investigation.

Question: Some of us are very much interested in trying to study experimentally the problem of whether or not the hypothesis concerning the four functions is tenable. We have a hypothesis by which, theoretically, we should be able to do this and to see whether or not people can be categorized into these four different pigeonholes, so to speak. In America there have been many attempts to find out whether people can be thought of as extraverts and introverts, and to the best of my knowledge there has never been any support for the idea, because most people are somewhere in between. What is your feeling about attempts at working on this hypothesis experimentally?

Dr. von Franz: I think you are absolutely right to go ahead with your experiment. Nobody tries simply to assert that this theory of types is true; we should have to test many millions of people statistically—something which has not been done. As you can see from my explanations, however, the diagnosis of type is very difficult, for people are often in stages where they are sure they are of a certain type, but you need the whole case history to know whether it is only a momentary stage of that person. For example, someone says that he is an extravert, but that means nothing; you have carefully to take the whole biography of that person to make a relatively safe diagnosis. Up till now we have had no absolutely safe, scientific foundation for our theory and we do not pretend to have.

My attitude toward this is that the idea of the four functions is an archetypal model for looking at things and that it has the advantage—and disadvantage—of all scientific models. Professor Pauli, the physicist, once said something which seems to me to be very convincing, namely, that no new theory, or no new fruitful invention in the field of science, has ever been put forth without the working of an archetypal idea. For instance, the ideas of three-dimensional or four-dimensional space are based on an archetypal representation which has always worked, to a certain degree, in a very productive way and has helped to explain a lot of phenomena. But then comes what Pauli calls the self-limitation of a theory, namely, that if one over-expands the idea to phenomena where it does not work, that same fruitful idea becomes an inhibition for further scientific progress. The idea of three-dimensional space, for example, is still completely valid for ordinary mechanics, and every carpenter and mason uses it when he makes a drawing or a plan, but if you try to over-expand it into micro-physics you go off the rails. So it can be said that it was an archetypal idea which originated, as can be clearly proved, in the scientific mind of Westerners through the dogma of the Trinity. Kepler, when he made his planetary models, said that space has three dimensions because of the Trinity! Or, take Descartes's idea of causality—saying that it was based on the fact that God never has whims but always proceeds in a logical manner and therefore everything must be causally connected.

All basic ideas, even of natural science, are archetypal models, but they work if one does not over-expand them. They work in a fruitful way if one does not force into them facts which do not fit. So I think the theory of the four functions has a kind of practical value, but it is not a dogma. Jung, in his books, very clearly puts it forward in this way, as a heuristical standpoint—a hypothesis by which you can find out things. We know now that in all scientific investigations we cannot do more than put forward thinking models, make models and see how far the facts fit, and if the facts do not coincide we have to correct the model. Sometimes we need not revise the whole thinking model; we simply say that it only applies in a certain area, and that as soon as one switches over to another area of facts, it becomes a distortion. I personally am convinced that we have not yet exhausted the fruitfulness of the model, but that does not mean that there are no facts which do not fit into it and might force us to revise it.

Question: Does an introverted feeling type experience introverted thinking, or is it always extraverted inferior thinking?

Dr. von Franz: If you are an introverted feeling type, you *can* also think introvertedly. You can naturally have all the functions all ways, but it won't be such a great problem, and there will not be much intensity of life in it. Jung has said that the hardest thing to understand is not your *opposite* type—if you have an introverted feeling it *is* very difficult to understand an extraverted thinking type—but the same functional type with the other attitude! It would be most difficult for an introverted feeling type to understand an extraverted feeling type. There one feels that one does not know how the wheels go round in that person's head; one cannot feel one's way into it. Such people remain to a great extent a puzzle and are very difficult to understand spontaneously. Here the theory of types is tremendously important practically, for it is the only thing which can prevent one from completely misunderstanding certain people. It gives a clue to the understanding of a person whose spontaneous reactions are a complete puzzle, whom you would, if you reacted spontaneously, misunderstand completely.

Question: What is the difference between inferior intuition and inferior feeling?

Dr. von Franz: Intuition is an irrational function which grasps facts, future possibilities and possibilities of evolution, but it is not a function of judgment. Inferior intuition might have presentiments about a war, or illnesses of other people, or of archetypal changes in the collective unconscious. Introverted intuition has sudden hunches about the slow transformation of the collective unconscious in the flow of time. Intuition presents facts with no valuation. Feeling is quite different. In Jungian terms, it is a rational function—*ratio:* order, calculation, reason—a function which establishes order and which judges, saying this is good and this is bad, this agreeable and this disagreeable to me. The inferior feeling of a thinking type would judge values and not represent facts. For example, an extraverted sensation type who neglected his intuition to a great extent had a recurring dream of poor people and laborers of a disagreeable type who broke into his house at night. He was terrified by this ever-recurring dream and began to go around in his circle of friends and at dinner parties saying there was absolutely nothing that could be done: he knew the Communists would win out. As he was a very able politician, this had a bad effect. This was a wrong kind of intuition, based on personal projection. That is an instance of inferior intuition. Someone with inferior feeling might suddenly start a lawsuit, convinced that he was fighting for the right and the good, but if someone else could shoot this conviction down, he would throw the whole thing over, including the lawsuit which he had himself begun.

The sudden change in his judgment would indicate the inferior feeling. People are very easily influenced when it is a question of their inferior function. Since it is in the unconscious, they can easily be made uncertain of their position, whereas in the realm of their superior function they generally know how to act when attacked; they have all their weapons ready and are broad-minded and flexible and feel strong. As soon as you feel strong you are quite willing to discuss things or to change your attitude, but where you feel inferior you get fanatical and touchy and are easily influenced. The expression on a friend's face can affect the feeling of a thinking type because his feeling is in the unconscious and therefore open to influence. Therefore, as I mentioned before, the extraverted thinking type can make very loyal friends but can suddenly turn against them. He may drop you one day like a hot potato, and

you don't know what happened! Somehow, something poison-
ous got into his system, someone said something, or even just
made a face when your name was mentioned! The feeling is unconscious. Such effects can only be cured when they are taken
up consciously. If you objected, in thinking terms, about his
policy in having the lawsuit, the extraverted thinking type
would be willing to discuss it and to ask your reasons. He would
be approachable and not influenced in a wrong way, while in
the realm of feeling he would break off suddenly and without
reason and without himself quite knowing why.

CHAPTER IV

The Role of the Inferior Function in Psychic Development

The inferior function is the door through which all the figures of the unconscious come into consciousness. Our conscious realm is like a room with four doors, and it is the fourth door by which the shadow, the animus or the anima, and the personification of the Self come in. They do not enter as often through the other doors, which is in a way self-evident: the inferior function is so close to the unconscious and remains so barbaric and inferior and undeveloped that it is naturally the weak spot in consciousness through which the figures of the unconscious can break in. In consciousness it is experienced as a weak spot, as that disagreeable thing which will never leave one in peace and always causes trouble. Every time one feels he has acquired a certain inner balance, a firm standpoint, something happens from within or without to throw it over again. This force always comes through the fourth door, which cannot be shut. The other three doors of the inner room can be closed. But on the fourth door the lock does not work, and there, when one is least prepared for it, the unexpected will come in again. Thank God, one might add, for otherwise the whole life process would petrify and stagnate in a wrong kind of consciousness. The inferior function is the ever-bleeding wound of the conscious personality, but through it the unconscious can always come in and so enlarge consciousness and bring forth a new attitude.

As long as one has not developed the other functions, the two auxiliary functions, they too will be open doors. In a person who has only developed one superior function, the two auxiliary functions will operate in the same way as the inferior function and will appear in personifications of the shadow, the animus and the anima. When one has succeeded in developing three functions, in locking three of the inner doors, the problem of the fourth door still remains, for that is the one that is apparently meant not to be locked. There one has to succumb; one has to suffer defeat in order to develop further.

In dreams, the inferior function relates to the shadow, the animus or the anima, and the Self, and it gives them a certain characteristic quality. For instance, the shadow in an intuitive type will often be personified by a sensation type. The inferior function is contaminated by the shadow in each type: in a thinking type it will appear as a relatively inferior or primitive feeling person, and so on. Thus, if in interpreting a dream one asks for a description of this shadow figure, people will describe their own inferior function. Then when one has become somewhat conscious of the shadow, the inferior function will give the animus or the anima figure a special quality. For example, the anima figure, if personified by a particular human being, will very often appear as a person of the opposite function. Again, when personifications of the Self appear, the same sort of thing will happen.

Another kind of personification, but one which naturally has to do with the shadow, occurs when the fourth function is contaminated by the lower levels of the social strata of the population or by the famous under-developed countries. It is a marvel how we in our superior arrogance look down on the 'under-developed countries' and project our inferior functions upon them! The under-developed countries are within ourselves! The inferior function often appears as a wild Negro or Indian. It is also frequently represented by exotic people of some kind:

Chinese, Russian, or whoever may possess something unknown to the conscious realm, as if it wanted to say, "it is as unknown to you as the Chinaman's psychology."

This social representation of the inferior function is particularly fitting in that this function tends to have, in its negative aspect, a barbaric character. It can cause a state of possession: if, for example, introverts fall into extraversion, they do so in a possessed and barbaric way. I mean barbaric in the sense of being unable to exert conscious control, being swept away, being unable to put a brake on, unable to stop. This kind of exaggerated, driven extraversion is rarely found in genuine extraverts, but in introverts it can be like a car without brakes that speeds on without the slightest control. An introvert may become highly disagreeable, pushy, arrogant, and shout so loudly that the whole room has to listen. Such inferior extraversion may suddenly pop out in this way when an introvert is drunk.

The introversion of the extravert is just as barbaric and possessed but not so visible to society. An extravert, if possessed by barbaric introversion, disappears right out of life. He goes mad in his own room. Extraverts who fall into their primitive introversion walk about looking very important, assuring everybody that they are having deep mystical experiences about which they cannot talk. In a self-important way they indicate they are now deeply steeped in active imagination and the process of individuation. One gets a strange feeling of a barbaric possession. If this happens in the form of Yoga or Anthroposophy there will be that same display of something mystical going on, of an unfathomable depth into which they have now dived. Actually, they are constantly tempted to switch back to their extraversion, which explains their over-emphasis on lack of time for contact with anybody. They would love to switch over to their extraversion and go to every party and dinner in town. So, defensively they say: "No, this is absolutely forbidden; now I am in the depths of the psyche." Very often in this phase people are sure that they *are* the type they now have to live. Extraverts who are in the phase where they should assimilate introversion will always swear that they are and always have been introverts and that it has always been an error to call them extraverts. In this way they try to help themselves get into the other side. If they try to express their inner experiences, they generally do so with over-excitement; they become terribly emotional and want to take the floor and have everybody listen. To them it is so tremendously unique and important.

This barbaric quality of the inferior function constitutes the great split of the human personality. One can thank God if one's opposite function is only personified in dreams by so-called primitives, for it is very often represented by stone-age figures or even by animals. In such a case, one can say that the inferior function has not even reached a primitively human level. The inferior function in that stage dwells, so to speak, in the body and can manifest itself only in physical symptoms or activities. When I see, for example, an introverted intuitive stretch himself in the sunshine with such marvelous enjoyment of his inferior function, I have the feeling that he is like a cat enjoying the sun; his sensation is still on the level of an animal.

In a thinking type feeling very often does not go beyond the dog level. It is more difficult to imagine that the feeling type thinks like an animal, but even that is true; they have a habit of making banal statements which one feels any cow could have made if it could speak. Dogs sometimes make helpless attempts to think. My own dog made an attempt and drew some terribly wrong conclusions. He always lay on my couch, and I used to chase him down; from that he concluded that I did not like him to sit on anything above the ground. So whenever I put him up on something, he became bewildered and thought he would be punished. He could not understand that it was only the couch and not every raised piece of furniture that was forbidden him. He had simply drawn the wrong conclusion! A dog has a halfway developed thinking function that tends to draw the wrong conclusions. I have often been struck by the fact that feeling types think in exactly the same way, for when you try to explain something to them they draw a general conclusion, some sweeping generalization that does not fit the situation in any way. Primitive thinking started in their heads, and they drew an amazingly unadapted conclusion that led to entirely wrong results. Thus one can often say that the thinking level of the feeling type is about on the dog's level: it is so helpless and stiff.

In most normal societies, people cover up their inferior func-

Persona

tion with a persona. One of the main reasons why one develops a persona is so as not to expose inferiorities, especially the inferiorities of the fourth function. It is contaminated with one's animal nature, one's unadapted emotions and affects.

When Jung founded the Psychological Club in Zürich, he wanted to find out how a group would work in which the inferior function would not be covered up, but where people would contact each other by it. The result was absolutely amazing. People who walked into this society from outside were shocked by the rude behavior and the absolutely unending quarrels this group displayed. I once visited the club many years ago. Until then I had never made a move toward becoming a member because I felt too shy. One day Jung said to me, "Do you not *want* to join the Psychological Club, or do you not *dare* join it?" I said I did not *dare* join it, but I would love to. So he said: "All right, I will be your godfather"—we need godfathers to get into the club—"but I'll wait first to see if you have a dream indicating the right moment has come." And what did I dream? I dreamt that a natural scientist, an old man who looked very much like Jung, had made up an experimental group to find out how animals of different species got along with each other. I came into the place; and there were aquariums with fishes in them, enclosures with tortoises, newts and such creatures, cages with birds and dogs and cats; and the old man was sitting in the middle, taking notes of how the animals behaved socially with each other. I discovered then that I was a flying fish in an aquarium and could jump out. I told my dream to Jung, and he said with a grin: "I think now you are mature enough to join the Psychological Club; you have got the central idea, its purpose."

In this rather humorous way the unconscious took up the idea: namely, that it is really a great problem when human beings contact each other, for in the inferior function one is a cat, another is a tortoise, and a third a hare—there are all those animals! In such a situation one must face the problem, for example, of maintaining one's own terrain. Many animal species have a tendency to 'own' a few meters of homeland and to defend it against all intruders. These complicated rituals of territorial defense build up again as soon as human beings join

— the inferior func. is covered up & plays havoc under the table.

together and put off the persona and try really to contact each other. Then one feels as if he were moving in the jungle: one must not step on this snake, or frighten that bird by making a quick movement, and things become very complicated. It has even led to the belief that psychology causes people to deteriorate in their social behavior, which to some extent is quite true.

At the C. G. Jung Institute, too, we are in a way much nastier and more difficult to get along with than, say, a society for breeding dogs or hares or a club for fishermen. There the social contact is in general on a much more conventional level, and it appears to be more civilized. But the truth is simply that at the institute and in the Psychological Club we tend not to cover up what is going on underneath. In most other societies or groups the inferior function is covered up and plays havoc under the table; underneath there are all these difficulties, but they are never brought up to the surface and discussed openly. The assimilation of the shadow and of the inferior function has the effect that people become socially more difficult and less conventional; this creates friction. On the other hand, it also creates a greater liveliness: it is never boring, there is always a storm in the teacup, and the group is very much alive instead of having just a kind of dull, polite surface. In the Psychological Club, for instance, the animal tendency to have one's territory became so strong that people started reserving seats. There was so-and-so's chair and you couldn't sit on it; that would be a major insult because so-and-so always sat there. I have noticed that there are also papers on certain chairs at the institute. There the dog or the cat so-and-so sits! That is a very good sign. It is a restoration of an original and natural situation.

It is amazing how deeply the inferior function can connect one to the realm of animal nature within oneself. Apart from the humorous way in which I have just described it, the inferior function is actually the connection with one's deepest instincts, with one's inner roots, and is, so to speak, that which connects us with the whole past of mankind. Primitive societies have dances with animal masks that are meant to connect the tribe with their ancestral ghosts, with the whole past of the tribe. We have, for the most part, lost such masked dances, though there is still the carnival as a remnant.

Once a person has experienced the *problem* of the functions, the next step in the process of psychic development is to assimilate the two auxiliary functions. One must not forget that the assimilation of these functions is such a difficult task that people generally spend a very long time at it. Sometimes people actually become a certain type, which was not their original type, for eight or ten years.

To assimilate a function means to live with that one function in the foreground. If one does a little cooking or sewing, it does not mean that the sensation function has been assimilated. Assimilation means that the whole adaptation of conscious life, for a while, lies on that one function. Switching over to an auxiliary function takes place when one feels that the present way of living has become lifeless, when one gets more or less constantly bored with oneself and one's activities. Generally it happens that one does not have to come to a theoretical conclusion about which function to switch to. The best way to know how to switch is simply to say: "All right, all this is now completely boring; it does not mean anything to me any more. Where in my past life is an activity that I feel I could still enjoy? An activity out of which I could still get a kick?" If a person then genuinely picks up that activity, he will see that he has switched over to another function.

I want to take up now the problem of establishing what I called in my first lecture the 'middle realm.' This becomes a crucial issue when a person reaches the stage of dealing seriously with his inferior function. The inferior function cannot be assimilated within the structure of the conscious attitude; it is too deeply implicated in and contaminated by the unconscious. It can be 'raised' somewhat, but in the process of raising it consciousness is pulled down. In the process of this dynamic interplay the middle realm is established.

Touching the inferior function resembles an inner breakdown at a certain crucial point of one's life. It has the advantage, however, of overcoming the tyranny of the dominant function in the ego complex. If someone has really gone through

The Lion (4th F.) eats mouse, cat, & dog & bones the one?

this transformation he can use his thinking function, if that is the appropriate reaction, or he can let intuition or sensation come into operation, but he is no longer possessed by one dominant function. The ego can take up a particular function and put it down, like a tool, in an awareness of its own reality outside the system of the four functions. This act of separation is achieved through encountering the inferior function. The inferior function is an important bridge to the experience of the deeper layers of the unconscious. Going to it and staying with it, not just taking a quick bath in it, effects a tremendous change in the whole structure of the personality.

Jung quotes again and again this old saying of the legendary alchemist and author, Maria Prophetissa: "One becomes two, two becomes three, and out of the third comes the one as the fourth." One becomes two: that is, first comes the development of the main function, then the assimilation of the first auxiliary. After that, consciousness assimilates a third; now there are three. But the next step does not consist of just adding another unit—one, two, three, and then four. Out of the third comes not the fourth but the One. Jung once told me in a private conversation that there is no fourth in the upper layer; it is like this:

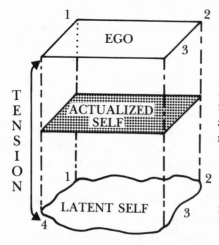

Field of naive ego-consciousness with three functions.

Middle field where the ego–Self relationship no longer functions autonomously but is only instrumental.

Preconscious totality with pre-formed four functions.

One can illustrate it in another way: there are a mouse, a cat, a dog and a lion. The first three animals can be domesticated if one treats them well, but then comes the lion. It refuses to be added as the fourth but eats up the others, so in the end there is only one animal left. The inferior function behaves like this: when it comes up, it eats the rest of the personality. The fourth becomes the One, for it is no longer the fourth; only one is left—i.e., a total psychic life phenomenon, no longer a function! Naturally, that is a simile and only gives a kind of illustration.

In his book *Mysterium Coniunctionis* (¶ 260), Jung quotes an alchemical text that mirrors the problem of the fourth function and the establishment of the middle ground. The text is called "Treatise of the Alchemist Aristotle addressed to Alexander the Great about the Philosophical Stone." It is probably of Arabic origin, and it appears translated into Latin in one of the early alchemical publications. The following recipe is given:

> Take the serpent, and place it in the chariot with four wheels, and let it be turned about on the earth until it is immersed in the depths of the sea, and nothing more is visible but the blackest dead sea. And there let the chariot with the wheels remain, until so many fumes rise up from the serpent that the whole surface (*planities*) becomes dry, and by desiccation sandy and black. All that is the earth which is no earth, but a stone lacking all weight. . . . [And when the fumes are precipitated in the form of rain,] you should bring the chariot from the water to dry land, and then you have placed the four wheels upon the chariot, and will obtain the result if you will advance further to the Red Sea, running without running, moving without motion [*currens sine cursu, movens sine motu*].

This is a very strange image. Take the wheels off the car and load them onto it! (It is interesting that one finds the same image in the *I Ching*. There it is sometimes said that one should take the wheels off the carriage. As far as I know, this Chinese image cannot have any direct connection with Western alchemy.) Jung then comments, The snake in alchemy is the symbol of Mercurius, the *prima materia,* the matter with which the process starts. Further on in the process Mercurius personifies a kind of nature spirit full of opposites. This snake is placed upon a carriage. The wheels are interpreted in the text as the wheels

of the elements and the car is called a spheric tomb, a round
tomb or sepulcher. The simile of the car in our text represents
the alchemical vessel in which the spirit of the unconscious is
contained. Jung says the symbolism in this passage describes the
essential phases of the opus: the snake of Hermes—the cold
side of nature, the unconscious—is caught in a round vessel
that is made of glass and represents the Cosmos as well as the
soul. From a psychological standpoint, such an image represents consciousness of both the outer and the inner worlds.
Putting the wheels onto the carriage indicates a cessation of all
four functions: one draws them in, so to speak. The later
transformation of these four wheels corresponds to the integration process through the transcendent function. The transcendent function unites the opposites, and, as alchemy shows, they
are ordered in a quaternio.

This alchemical symbol does not minimize the problem of the
fourth function, but it points to a solution. The ego assimilates
its first function and then is content for a while. After a time it
assimilates a second function and lives contentedly once more.
It has pulled up both from the unconscious. Then it pulls up a
third to the plane of consciousness. Now three functions are
assimilated on the upper, civilized level upon which we try normally to live. But one cannot bring the fourth function up to
this same level. On the contrary, if one tries too hard, the fourth
function will pull ego-consciousness down to a completely primitive level. One may identify with it and its impulses absolutely;
then there will occur those sudden switches in which people
suddenly drop down to an animal level.

I have referred to the film *The Blue Angel* in which this problem was represented: a college professor suddenly switches over
to his inferior feeling function and becomes a circus clown, being caught by admiration for a vamp-like woman in a cabaret.
But that is certainly not the *assimilation* of the fourth function.
One can drop down to a low animal level, if one wants, and live
out the inferior function in a concrete form without having
assimilated it in any way. In such a case one simply loses the
whole upper structure of the former personality. People who
have a great primitive courage for life can do this. When they
touch the fourth function they suddenly switch wholeheartedly

over into it. Jung tells of the case of a man who lived as a very re-spectable businessman until he was sixty. He had a family, a good business, and everything else, but then he became sleep-less and restless and unhappy for a few months. One night he sprang up in bed, shouting: "I have it!" His wife woke up and asked: "What?" "I have it, I am a bum! That's what I am!" He im-mediately left his wife and family and his business, spent all his money and drank himself to death. That was certainly coura-geous, but rather a drastic solution of the problem! He suddenly fell into the inferior side of his personality and forgot every-thing else.

The fourth function is always life's great problem: if I don't live it, I am frustrated and half-dead and everything is boring; if I live it, it is of such a low level that I cannot use it, unless I have the pseudo-courage of this man. Most people do not have that courage; others would have it but they see that this is no solu-tion either. So what does one do? At that moment this alchem-ical recipe comes into place: namely, the effort to deal with the fourth function by putting it into a spherical vessel, by giving it a frame of fantasy. One can get on not by living the fourth func-tion in a concrete outer or inner way, but by giving it the possibility of a fantasy expression, whether in writing or paint-ing or dancing or in any other form of active imagination. Jung found that active imagination was practically the only means for dealing with the fourth function.

In the choice of the means of active imagination one can see how the inferior function comes into effect. An intuitive type, for instance, will generally have a strong desire to fix his active imagination in clay or in stone, making it materially visible in some way. Otherwise it will not seem real, and the inferior func-tion will not come in. Jung, being an intuitive, discovered it first by the need to build little clay and stone castles, and from that experience he discovered the problem that is constellated by the fourth function. The rare form of dancing I have usually seen when feeling is the fourth function. Sometimes thinking types, when they have to assimilate their feeling function, have a genuine wish to express it by dancing in certain primitive rhythms. Inferior feeling can also express itself in very colorful paintings, color in general expressing strong feeling moods. A

— the 5th essence) (or
4 = the one)
— "Quin tessentia" —   *Marie-Louise von Franz*
philosopphers stone

sensation type will conceive weird fiction stories, such as I described earlier, or wild fantastic novels into which intuition can run. When the problem comes up of choosing the means for assimilating the unconscious psychological problem by fantasizing, the choice is generally connected with the inferior function.

When one reaches the stage of dealing decisively with the fourth function, it becomes impossible to stay on the upper level, but one may also not wish to drop down to the lower. So the middle area becomes the only possible solution. This middle ground, which is neither on the upper nor the lower level, is established through fantasizing in the specific form of active imagination. At this moment one transmits, as it were, his feeling of life into an inner center, and the four functions remain only as instruments which can be used at will, taking them up and putting them down again. The ego and its conscious activity are no longer identical with any of the functions. This is what the alchemical text represents by putting the four wheels upon the car. There is a complete standstill in a kind of inner center, and the functions do not act automatically any more. You can bring them out at will, as for instance an airplane can let down the wheels in order to land and then draw them in again when it has to fly. At this stage the problem of the functions is no longer relevant; the functions have become instruments of a consciousness which is no longer rooted in them or driven by them. It has its basis of operation in another dimension, a dimension that can only be created by the world of imagination. That is why Jung calls this the transcendent function. This right kind of imagination creates the uniting symbols.

This coincides with the alchemical symbolism that speaks of the problem of the four elements—water, fire, air and earth. In our text they are represented as the wheels that have to be integrated. Then comes the fifth essence, which is not another additional element, but is, so to speak, the essence of all four and yet none of the four; it is the four in one. To the four comes a fifth thing which is not the four but is something beyond them and consists of them all. That is what the alchemists called the fifth essence, the *quintessentia* or the philosopher's stone. It means a consolidated nucleus of the personality which is no longer identified with any of the functions. This is a stepping out, so to speak, of identification with one's own consciousness and with one's own unconscious, and dwelling, or trying to dwell, on this middle plane. From then on, as the text says, one moves without movement, runs without running (*currens sine cursu, movens sine motu*). After this stage is reached, another kind of development begins. In alchemy, as well as in the development of the personality, the solution to the problem of the functions is the first step, but it is enormously difficult to get even as far as that.

(A period of questions and answers follows.)

Question: What happens in a human life when this middle sphere is attained?

Dr. von Franz: What does someone look like when he has detached his ego-awareness, or his ego-consciousness, from identification with certain functions? I think the nearest and most convincing example would be in some descriptions of the behavior of Zen Buddhist Masters. It is said that the door of the inner house is closed, but the Master meets everybody and every situation and everything in the usual manner. He continues in everyday life, participating in it in a normal way. If people come to be taught, he will teach them with feeling. If a difficult problem is put before him, he can think about it. If it is the moment to eat, he will eat, and if it is the moment to sleep, he will sleep; he uses his sensation function in the right way. When it is a question of seeing through the other person in a flash of intuition, or through the situation, he will do that. He will not, however, be inwardly bound to the ego functions he uses in meeting the particular situation. He will have lost a certain kind of childish eagerness to meet things. If you present people who are still identical with their thinking with a thinking problem, they go right into it. This is necessary, because if they do not learn to be right in it they will never learn to think properly and appropriately. But after the transformation, if you present them with a thinking problem they remain inwardly detached from it, though they can apply their thinking to the problem: they can stop thinking from one minute to another without having to continue it. It is difficult to bring examples because there are very few people who have reached that stage, but there are very good descriptions of being detached from one's own conscious functions in these Zen Buddhist examples.

Question: Could you describe the difference between the kind of discipline that one practices in Jungian analysis, as compared, say, with that of the Zen Buddhist monk?

Dr. von Franz: There are analogies, but I would say that it is not the same thing. I think that our way of trying to approach the problem of the inferior function imposes a kind of discipline on all individuals which has an analogy in the monastic life, not only in the East but also in the West. For instance, remaining with the difficulty for a long time, giving up other occupations in order to have enough time and energy for this main problem, practicing a kind of asceticism. But the monastic life, whether in the East or in the West, is a collectively organized affair. You have to get up at a certain time, do a certain work, obey the abbot and so on; in contrast to that, the discipline that comes upon an individual within the process of individuation is imposed purely from within. There are no outer rules, and therefore the thing is much more individual. If you let it happen spontaneously instead of forcing it from outside by organized discipline, you will see that the discipline is completely different from person to person.

For a while I analyzed two men who were friends; one was an introverted thinking type and the other an extraverted feeling type. The extravert's discipline was very severe, for even if he drank a glass of wine or stayed at a dinner party half an hour too long, he had the most awful dreams. Sometimes both would receive invitations, and the typical introvert would say he had no time, but promptly dreamt that he had to go to the party. His friend, on the other hand, who had received the same invitation, had the dream (naturally he had already decided on his costume and knew which lady he would invite to come with him) telling him he should not go! No party, stay at home! It was really amusing to see how it was just as great an agony for the introvert to go to a party as it was sad for the other poor chap to stay away. Sometimes they would exchange notes and say, "Isn't it really nasty! Now I would like to go and may not, and you hate going but your dreams say 'Go!'" So you see there is a kind of discipline, but it is invisible and very precisely adjusted. That is the advantage of our way of dealing with the problem; you get your very appropriate, private discipline—invisible to the outer world, but very disagreeable.

Question: You have given several alternatives, one of which is the achievement of the middle ground, which seems to be extremely rare, so that in fact very few people get this far. Another alternative is where the roaring lion comes up, and, I assume, some degree of illness follows. Is there an alternative between these two?

Dr. von Franz: Yes. You have a great many people who from time to time experience the problem of the inferior function—what I have spoken of as getting into the hot bath and then jumping out of it again. Afterward they more or less go on with their three functions, constantly slightly uncomfortable on account of the non-integrated fourth. When things get too bad they dive in a bit, but as soon as they feel better, they get out again. On principle, they remain in their trinitarian world where the fourth is the devil who remains in a corner of their life. People who stick in this phase never quite understand what Jung means by the problem of the fourth, and they never quite understand what individuation really means. They remain in the conventional former world of identifying with consciousness. Many people who have even undergone a Jungian analysis do not get further than those brief visits into the fourth realm and then talking about it to others—not really trying to stay in it—because it is hellishly difficult to achieve.

Question: How does the inferior function connect with the collective evil?

Dr. von Franz: As long as you do not really get into this stage there remains what I call the devil in the corner. This is only the personal devil, the personal inferiority of an individual, but with it collective evil comes in as well. The little open door of each individual's inferior function is what contributes to the sum of collective evil in the world. You could observe that very easily in Germany when the devil slowly took over the situation in the Nazi movement. Every German I knew at that time who fell for Nazism did so on account of his inferior function. The feeling type got caught by the stupid arguments of the party doctrine; the intuitive type got caught by his dependence on money. He could not give up his job and did not see how he could deal with the money problem, so he had to stay in it despite the fact that he did not agree, and so on. The inferior function was in each personal realm the door where some of this collective evil could accumulate. Or, you could say that each one who had not worked on his inferior function contributed to this general disaster—in a small way—but the sum of millions of inferior functions constitutes an enormous devil! Propaganda against the Jews was very cleverly made up in that respect. For example, the Jews were insulted as being destructive intellectuals, which completely convinced all the feeling types—a projection of inferior thinking. Or they were accused of being reckless money-makers; that completely convinced the intuitive, for they were his inferior sensation, and now one knew where the devil was. The propaganda used the ordinary suspicions that people had against others on account of their inferior function. So you can say that behind each individual the fourth function is not just a little kind of deficiency; the sum of these is really responsible for a tremendous amount of trouble.

Question: Is there a moral issue involved in individuation? Is it a question of perfection in a strictly moral sense?

Dr. von Franz: The process of individuation is an ethical problem, and someone without any morality would get stuck right at the beginning. But the word "perfection" is not appropriate. That is a Christian ideal which does not quite coincide with our experience of the process of individuation. Jung says that the process seems not to tend toward perfection but toward completeness. This means, I think, that you cannot get the thing up to the upper level (of the diagram), but *you* have to come *down*, and that means a relative lowering of the level of the personality. If you are in the middle, the one side is not as dark and the other not quite as bright, and there is more a tendency to constitute a kind of completeness which is neither too light nor too dark. But one has to sacrifice a certain amount of striving for moral perfection in order to avoid building up too black a counter-position. It is ethical, but not idealistic. One has to give up the illusion that one can produce something perfect in the human realm.

Question: Would you say that propaganda is mainly a field for the inferior function?

Dr. von Franz: Yes, if it is the type of propaganda that is built up with the object of engendering emotion. Someone practicing such a low type of propaganda would know that it is not by reasonable talk that one gets the masses, but by arousing emotion. Emotion can be aroused in everyone at the same time if you bring up the inferior function, because as I said before, that is the emotional function. Therefore, if you speak to intellectuals you must arouse primitive feelings! If you speak to university professors, you must not use scientific language because in that field their minds are clear and they will see through all the snares in your speech. If you want to get a lie across, you must substantiate your lie with a lot of feeling and emotion. Since university professors will on the average have inferior feeling, they will fall for that at once. Hitler had the art of doing this. His speeches show that he talked quite differently to different groups, and he knew very well how to wake up the inferior function. A man who had been present at several of his speeches told me that he did it through his intuition, by feeling his way into the situation. At times, Hitler would at first be quite uncertain. He would try out his themes like a pianist, mentioning a little of this and a little of that. He would be pale and nervous, and his SS men would get all worked up because the Führer did not seem to be in form. But he was just trying out the ground. Then he would notice that if he brought up a particular subject, it would arouse emotion, so then he would just go full tilt for that! That's the demagogue. When he feels that inferior side, he knows where the complexes are, and that is what he goes for. One must argue in a primitive, emotional way, the way in which the inferior function would argue. Hitler did not think that out. It was the fact that he was caught in his own inferiority which gave him that talent.

Dr. von Franz: I have been asked whether emotion and feeling are connected? The answer is, only when it is a case of inferior feeling. Emotion and feeling are connected in a thinking type. I think of the national differences between French and Germans. The German language has many words for feeling that are confused with emotion, while the French word for feeling, *sentiment,* conveys nothing of emotion, not a shade of it. In general the French, as a nation, have more differentiated feeling, so to them it is not emotional. This is why the French always make fun of German feelings. They say: "Oh, the Germans, with their heavy feeling—beer and singing and *'Oh Heimatland'*—all that sentimental stuff." A Frenchman has *sentiment,* a clear-cut thing with no wishy-washiness about it. There you have an example of the feeling type condemning the inferior feeling of a nation whose superiority is not in feeling. The Germans think much better, but their feeling is rather primitive, warm and full of the atmosphere of the stable, but also full of explosives!

Question: Would you equate the transcendent function with *'gestalten'*?

Dr. von Franz: It is different from what generally is used in *'gestalten'* or what is used when you let people just fantasize freely. Here it is fantasizing with ego-consciousness taking its standpoint. This activity is driven by the urge toward individuation. When this urge is still unconscious, it is simply that element of constant dissatisfaction and restlessness which nags people till they reach a higher level again and again in life. The *principium individuationis* is naturally this transcendent function, but in Jungian psychology one does not let it just bite one till one has to take the next step; one turns toward it directly and tries to give it form by expressing it through active imagination. And that, in a way, then leads to an evolution which transcends the problem of the four functions; the constant battle of the four functions then comes to rest.

Question: Is this stage, then, a permanent condition of active imagination?

Dr. von Franz: Yes, this is the plane on which active imagination takes control. With the inner nucleus of consciousness you stay in the middle place; you no longer identify with what goes on in the upper or lower planes. You stay within your active imagination, so to speak, and you have the feeling that this is where your life process goes on. For instance, on the one plane you very often notice synchronistic events happening, and on the other are the dreams, but *you keep your consciousness turned toward the events which happen on the middle plane, on the events which evolve within your active imagination.* This becomes the function with which you move along through life. The other planes still exist for you, but you are not centered in them. The center of gravity shifts away from the ego and its functions into an interim position, into attending to the hints of the Self. For instance, a Chinese text which describes the process says consciousness is then in a position like a cat watching a mousehole —not too dull and not too tense. If a cat is too tense, it gets cramps and misses the mouse; if it is too dull, the mouse will walk out and the cat will miss it. This kind of (half-dimmed) conscious attention is turned toward the inner process.

Question: Has Dr. Jung applied this theory of functions to his ideas about the Trinity and quaternity in his studies on religion?

Dr. von Franz: Put briefly, I would answer in the affirmative. That is, the problem of the third and the fourth in religious symbolism connects with the problem of the four functions. It connects as the archetypal model connects with the single case. To refer to the drawing I gave you in the first lecture, the archetypal constellation would be at the base of the psyche; this is the structural tendency to develop four functions. You can find this archetype in mythologies of four persons, in the four directions of the compass, in the four winds, in the four angels at the four corners of the world. It is in Christian symbolism also. For instance, there are the four evangelists, where three are animals and one a human being. There are also the four sons of Horus, three of whom have animal heads and one a human head. Those are manifestations of a basic structural archetype in the human psyche, of the disposition in a human being which, as soon as he tries to cast a model of a total existence—a model of the total cosmic world or of total human life—tends to use a fourfold model. The choice just naturally falls upon a fourfold model more often than on any other. In China, it is to be found every-where. The fourfold mandalas always arise from an impulse to cast a model of total existence, where people do not want to face a single fact but want a mapping out of general phenomena. It would therefore be an inherent, inborn, structural disposition in the human psyche to use such fourfold models for totalities.

The problem of the four functions in the consciousness of an individual would be a secondary product of this more basic model. It is not advisable to project the factors of the un-conscious structure upon the field of consciousness or to use the factors of the conscious functions to explain the archetypal structure. The problem of the four functions in the conscious-ness of an individual is *one* of the manifestations of these more general archetypal dispositions. If, for instance, you try to ex-plain the model of the four mountains in the four directions of the world in China, or the four winds in the four corners of the world, by saying that one must be thinking and the other *must* be another function, you never get anywhere. It simply does not click! The archetype of the quaternio as a model of the total situation is more general than the four functions. It would therefore be wrong-headed to reduce the dogma of the Trinity and the problem of the fourth person of the Trinity, whether the virgin Mary or the devil, to the problem of functions. Rather turn it the other way round; it is a general archetypal problem, but in the individual it assumes the form of the four functions. For example, in the Christian religion the devil is the symbol of absolute evil in the Godhead, but it would be very presumptuous if you accorded your inferior thinking or inferior feeling such a great honor as to call it the devil in person! That would be rather an inflated explanation of your inferiorities. Just as you could not say that your three relatively developed functions were identical with the Trinity. As soon as you put it as bluntly as that, you see how ridiculous the idea would be. Nevertheless, you *can* say that there is a connection, since evil, negativism and destructiveness do connect with the inferior function in the individual.

I can give you an instance of how this connection operates. An intuitive person had to send me a letter with some very agreeable news for me, but she was very jealous and mislaid the letter. Now did her inferior function make her mislay the letter with the good news for me, or was it her intriguing jealous shadow? It was both! The intriguing jealous shadow got her via the inferior function. You can never pin down such a person; you can only say: "Oh, that's your inferior sensation, don't let's mention it again." But it is typical enough that the shadow, the negative impulse, sneaks into the inferior function. I remember the case of a man, a feeling type, who was terribly jealous because a woman in whom he was interested had a tremendous transference to Jung. So this gentleman felt snubbed by her. She just wouldn't look at him, and that cut him to the heart. He could not get over it for a long time. Finally he wrote a book against Jungian psychology, full of errors and misquotations, in which he put forth a 'better new philosophy.' Now you can see, on the feeling level—his superior function—this man could not do such a nasty thing: he could not attack Jung directly as a person because his feeling was too differentiated. He saw clearly that Jung, who could not help this woman's transference, had nothing to do with the business. So his feeling remained decent. But his inferior thinking picked the motivation—which was rotten jealousy and nothing else—and produced the most amazing junk. He was not even able to copy out the quotations properly because he had been blinded and swept away by a shadow impulse. Shadow impulses, destructive impulses, jealousy, hatred, and so on generally get one via the inferior function, because that is a weak spot; that is where we are not in control of ourselves, not constantly aware of the operations of our actions.

In this corner, therefore, any destructive or negative tendencies attack, and there you could say that the devil has to do with the fourth function because he gets people through it. If you speak medieval language, you can say that the devil wants to destroy people and will always try to get you by your inferior function. The fourth door of your room is where angels can come in, but also devils!

PART TWO

James Hillman
The Feeling Function

CHAPTER I

Historical Introduction

A function is something that performs, operates, acts. It is a process going on through a certain period of time. The word "function" comes from *fungi, fungor,* to perform, and its Sanscrit root (*bhunj*) refers to "enjoy." Enjoying is still associated with *functus* in Latin. The exercise and performance of a function is something to enjoy, as a pleasant or healthy activity, as the operation of one's powers in any sphere of action.

Jung uses the terms "function" and "organ" rather as one does in physiology: an organ performs the functions specific to it. But Jung also insists that a function precedes its organ or, as Aristotle said in his *Ethics,* we become good by doing good; we develop a characteristic structure through habitual performance. I mention this view of a function so that as we proceed we may have in mind a relatively unified, relatively consistent and habitual pattern of performance which enjoys itself in its activity, a pattern that likes to be exercised.

Because functions can be conceived in this developmental way, they are appropriately conceived in Jung's psychology as the functions of consciousness. They belong to the development of the conscious personality, forming part of the ego, its consistency, its habits, unity and memory, its characteristic way of performing. Functions are part of the *intentionality* of consciousness, showing how it operates in regard to itself and others, how it imposes its intentions and meanings and expresses its character.

Functions are therefore later phenomena than complexes in the growth of the individual. Complexes also function and have reactions and habits—push the same button, get the same response. Functions, however, are classically conceived in Jungian thought as aspects of the *ego*-complex, even if thinking or feeling may be associated with anima or animus, shadow or mother-complex, etc. Even the inferior function, which may reach to the depths of the archaic unconscious soul, is yet conceived from the viewpoint of ego-consciousness as potentially a function of the ego. This is evidently not true for the complexes and their archetypal cores. They are never conceived as operations of the ego. Complexes form the theoretical substrate of the psyche, and they can, of course, dominate the four psychological functions. For instance, one's feeling function may be highly determined by the mother-complex so that all one's feeling responses, values and judgments reflect the personal mother or are in contradiction to her. Or, one's intuitions may be mother-dominated, a nose for the nasty; or everything that one smells, eats, notices, touches may have a sexual-erotic thrill.

Functions as ways of operating differ, too, from contents. One may have feelings, thoughts, perceptions, but only a conscious organization can perform with them. A thought may come through the mind, but this is not thinking; one may sit under sad feelings all day but this is not feeling.

Let us conceive these functions as four modes of organizing and suffering life. Let us follow Jung further in assuming that these four modes are basic to the psyche and that there are no more than four. They would then be archetypally given with psychic structure, necessary and sufficient. Here, Jung would seem to be re-expressing an ancient metaphor of the fourfold root. This idea has often been brought forward as a basic principle in accounting for human nature. Man was said to be composed of four basic elements (earth, air, water and fire), humors

and temperaments (melancholic, choleric, sanguine and phleg-
matic). Attempts to equate the functions with these older principles do not quite work—feeling with water or with phlegm—
since each age has its appropriate ciphers for expressing this archetypal metaphor, and translations of it violate the context of
the symbol. Nor should we elaborate the metaphor into an all-
inclusive meta-psychological system where all sorts of images
can be fitted: e.g., feeling is represented by red colors and by the
chest region of the body, or by one of the four seasons, directions, times of day and Gospel writers, etc. Four is a necessary
symbol for a complete picture of the psyche, but each set of
fours is different and they are not interchangeable.

Cultural history shows heights in the appreciation of feeling
in Greece and Rome, even if social historians often point to
slavery, cruelty and the oppression of foreigners and of women
in ancient civilization in order to drive home the message that
Christianity brought in new and higher feeling values. Nevertheless, Greek and Roman thought shows concern with feeling
matters, whether in the conduct of life and the city, in matters of
human relationships, or in aesthetics. Above all, their differentiated pantheon of divine figures offered an archetypal background to many forms of feeling expression. Because the Gods
were many, the relation to them could not be encompassed in
only one ritual or through one creed. Polytheism gave the
multiplicity of complexes in the psyche a background for finding values and relating to many aspects of life, which we now
more narrowly condemn as perverse, irreligious, obscene and
inhuman. One simply had to appreciate the feeling claims of
the different Gods and find ways to relate to this archetypal
background of existence, whereas in a book-religion with a code
and a catechism and a credo many feeling problems are taken
care of without reflection.

Later, in the late middle ages, for example, a great deal was
understood about courtly love and mystical love. Catholic doctrine and monastic life encouraged deep-going self-reflection of
feeling life but, unfortunately, too often in the context of goodness and sin. Then, in the Renaissance, other aspects of feeling
came to the fore. The presentation of passions and emotions occurred through painting and sculpture, and the analysis of feel-

ing was a dominant theme of the writers. Love was a favorite theme during the fifteenth to seventeenth centuries, and, as the fine arts, music and literature developed into the forms we are now familiar with, a differentiation of feeling took place, casting this function into the accepted modes we now consider to be ethically correct, aesthetically pleasing and politically decent. In other words, our notion of "good feeling" in taste or conduct, or of deep "religious feeling," is very much the result of a historical process.

During the eighteenth century novelists and poets began their subtle and exhaustive descriptions of feeling states, and during the Romantic period which immediately followed appeared such statements as "feeling is all" and "beauty is truth." There is little of this emphasis today in either philosophy or psychology, while literature concerns itself more with the coarser passions in a narrower style, or with the apathetic absence of feeling in an art of depersonalization. Psychotherapy and some new theology seem to be the areas where feeling today is given theoretical place and even worshiped as the goal of life.

For a history of the feeling function *as a concept* we must turn to the philosophers. The background of psychology is philosophy; the two fields have only recently been separated. Plato, Aristotle, the Scholastics, Descartes, Spinoza, Hume, Kant—all take up the affective life and make it an important part of their philosophies. In fact, the old humanistic tradition concerns itself with an understanding of feeling, and the modern academic split between science and the humanities turns principally on the feeling function, which is not appropriate to science as it is today defined. Academic and clinical psychology run the danger, in their urge to be scientific and objective, of losing their connection to human feeling when they neglect their historical roots in philosophy and theology. The background of clinical psychology is only secondarily the psychopathology of illnesses, only secondarily the scientific or medical approach of clinical work. To understand the feeling function we must begin long before modern psychiatry's descriptions of its peculiar vicissitudes; we must begin with the humanism of the moral philosophers and essayists, the novelists and dramatists, the theologians and mystics, rather than with contemporary psychologists.

The concept of feeling as a separate faculty of the psyche appears in modern thought in the faculty psychology of the eighteenth century. At that time, the psyche was divided into three faculties: thinking, willing and feeling. Perhaps historians of ideas will one day tell us more about the birth of feeling in the eighteenth century, for it was in the air of the time: introspective Pietism, Rousseau, the Sentimental Novels and the word "sentimental," the culture and manners of courts, of cities, of *salons* and coffeehouses, the refinement of written language and interest in accents and tones of speech, the development of music, the origins of Romanticism, the enthusiasm of political revolutionaries and religious reformers. During this same period, the concept of feeling as a separate faculty of the psyche enters psychology as an equal in the trinity of thinking, willing and feeling, a tri-partite division that still provides the framework for university courses in psychology on the European continent today. The term "feeling," to describe a separate faculty, was first introduced by Moses Mendelssohn in 1766. Already in 1755 he had written: *"Wir fühlen nicht mehr sobald wir denken"* ("We no longer feel as soon as we think"—*Philosophische Schriften,* I, 9). We shall see in Jung's description of the feeling function an essentially identical statement.

"Feelings" as the word for emotions, sympathies and susceptibilities enters English in 1771. This was a time when feelings were of huge importance, somewhat as today. Everyone spoke of his states of soul as feelings. New words were preempted by the feeling function. "Interesting" and "bored" joined the language, the former via Sterne's *Sentimental Journey* in 1768. Other eighteenth-century contributions to feeling vocabulary are *"ennui, chagrin, home-sickness, diffidence, apathy,* while the older words, *excitement, agitation, constraint, embarrassment, disappointment,* come to be applied to inner experiences" (L. P. Smith, *The English Language,* London, n.d.). As Pearsall Smith points out, it is not that people before the eighteenth century had no home-sickness or apathy, had no feeling and emotions and sentiments, but this was the time in psychological

[handwritten margin notes at top: "feeling descriptions transferred from outer events to inner ones — affectivity became the lowest division — equated to the dark passions a lowest strata (co-vibrational..."]

history when consciousness began to reflect upon feeling as such. This is also the time, the end of the eighteenth century, that the first textbooks were written with "psychology" in their titles. The difference between the older vocabulary of feeling and that of the modern period (out of which psychology was born) consists in the transfer of feeling descriptions from outer events (as "baleful," "sinister," "benign") to inner events. When we say an event is amusing or interesting today, we generally refer to feelings that take place within ourselves. (See: O. Barfield, *History in English Words,* London, 1953.) The origins of modern academic psychology are quite closely bound with introspection and the transfer of feeling from an outer to an inner world. Gestalt psychology has tried during the last fifty years to place feelings again "outside" in the landscape as objective qualities of the scene, arising from the "feel" of the lines and colors and forms.

The separation of affective experience and the attempts to organize and classify it, mainly through the introspective method, are a great contribution of German and, to a lesser extent, French and British-Scottish psychology. The tri-partite division suggested by Mendelssohn took on authority as worked out by Tetens and then by Kant in his *Anthropology.* Once the idea had been presented by Kant, it became official and orthodox, to last the centuries. This third division included all sorts of affectivity—emotion, sensation, pleasure and pain, sensing of the good, moral and aesthetic values, sentiments, passions: whatever did not belong either to thinking or willing.

Unfortunately, this division became absorbed by an older model still dreaming in the psyche, the tri-partite division in Plato's *Republic*; or, we might say that a trinitarian model for the hierarchical description of consciousness is a Western archetype that appears in different forms in different centuries. The influence of the Platonic division (Head and Gold, Heart and Silver, Liver and Bronze) was distinctly negative for the faculty of feeling. Affectivity became the lowest, blurring its edges and confusing its realm with that of the dark passions and the lowest strata of sex, sin, the irrational and feminine and materialistic. Feeling, which is not all the same as passion or emotion, can and

[handwritten margin notes at bottom: "feminine, materialistic — gestalt therapy tries to place feeling outside as objective"]

does become passionate and emotional owing to the collective repression and consequent lack of differentiation.

The collective repression of the affective side of the psyche in our history and the return of the repressed—today waving the banners of "feeling" in the church, in teach-in's, in groups, in advertising, wherever—have left us with a sense of loss. Loss is the main characteristic of feeling just now; we are at a loss, not knowing how to feel, where to feel, why to feel, or even if we feel. There is loss of individual feeling style and form, as if an ability has got crippled. We are left with what T. S. Elliot calls in his *Four Quartets* "the general mess of imprecision of feeling,/ Undisciplined squads of emotion," so that our task may also be described by another passage from the same work of Eliot's:

Only the fight to recover what has been lost
And found and lost again and again: and now under conditions
That seem unpropitious.

So much is feeling the problem of the times that one could preposterously assert that the whole field of psychotherapy resulted from inadequacies of the feeling function. Our personal feeling problems are partly a collective result of the ages of repression, which have by no means been lifted by the confused enthusiasms of the eighteenth century nor by the pornographic delights of the mid-twentieth. Our feeling problems are collective problems, and we need new fantasies for them. To deal with them only directly, with a new doctrine of feeling and a revolution in its name, is not enough. The shibboleths of the age are *connect, relate, be human, be sincere, feel*—but how? And what do these slogans mean?

Academic psychologists, with a few outstanding exceptions, have preferred to let feeling alone, justifying their neglect with arguments that feeling cannot be analyzed. Feeling, they say (and this is particularly true of the German schools, who in spite of their arguments keep on writing about feeling), is a flow which cannot be cut up and looked at. Even asking questions, the first step in any inquiry, stops feeling. They point to common life where if one is asked, "How does it feel?" the answer in words is already different from the feeling phenomenon. The application of analytical intellect to feeling destroys the very thing under examination; it melts before one's eyes. So—this argument runs—feeling is better left in the dark as an underground force, to be felt and not formulated.

Because there is little objective evidence to consider, the study of feeling seems such a personal matter. Psychologists are aware of this, and three times in this century there have been extraordinary symposia on Feelings and Emotions. The first, the Wittenberg symposium, was held in 1927, and many illustrious psychologists—Alfred Adler, Bekhterev, Janet, Pieron, Brett—took part, each giving his view of feeling and of emotion. Again, in 1948, there was a similar symposium on Feelings and Emotions, organized through the University of Chicago. Margaret Mead, Carl Rogers, David Katz, Gesell, French, Buytendijk, Gardner Murphy and a score of others each presented a theory of feeling and of emotion, and research on every possible aspect. Now, twenty years have passed, and the third such symposium took place at Loyola in the autumn of 1968. It included a synopsis and the implications of Jung's views which I presented. For anyone wanting to examine this field more academically, the three volumes representing these symposia are basic.

But the study of feeling leads outside psychology and into social history and biography, family life and friendships, literature, poetry, politics and diplomacy—all places where the psychologist usually feels nervous. I have collected the academic books in this field for years—my indirect way to feeling—and I can report that there is little fantasy in this stuff, and it is leadenly dull reading.

Jung has given us one clue to feeling that is far from dull because it pertains to our actual psychic life and to its basis in the complexes. If the complexes are defined as groups of feeling-toned ideas, then one component of every complex is feeling and one way into every complex is via its feelings. We can discover the complex through dream imagery, through sensations and memories, through projections, through ideas and their analysis—but also through feelings. The approach through feeling applies as well to dreams, which are expressions of the complexes. The selecting and appreciating of dream values, as well as the feelings released through dreams, are ways of elaborating the complexes; feeling is a *via regia* to the unconscious, not only in our personal lives, but to the larger archetypal dominants which make their impersonal claims upon us through feelings. This implies that our feelings, seemingly so closely intimate and personally "ours," also have their archetypal impersonal aspect, deserving recognition on that level.

Let me stress this again: feelings are not only personal; they reflect historical and universal phenomena. They are common and collective. A need that seems so personal may express the need common to our relationship, common to the family as a group, common to a group of society, and even common to the age. Our feelings are not "ours" only. We partake in them, as for instance national feelings and religious feelings. In this sense they are not only something "in" us, but also something we are "in," and which the feeling function can help us sort through. The belief that feelings are "mine," personal and revelatory of who I am and where I stand and what I want, is very much an illusion of the feeling-ego. Just as the sensations of taste and smell vary little between people, or the thoughts in the minds and the processes of thinking vary little among members in the collective society, so too with feelings. The differentiation of individualized feeling into an original style is as rare as originality in any function. Because therapists sometimes neglect the impersonal collectivity of feelings, analysands are led to believe that if they can only express their feelings fully they can find honesty and become centered. The feeling function is the instrument with which we sort out the genuine and the spurious —no easy task, maybe not even possible. In any event, we should not burden this function with the entire weight of self-discovery and expect that feeling alone will make us genuine and authentic persons.

There are other ways to depth besides "deep" feelings. Because feeling has been so blown up recently, people have come to take it as the panacea for therapy. But I shall be proceeding in a different way: not a therapy through feeling but a therapy of feeling, an attempt to bring awareness to the ways that feeling functions.

Ideally, one should have a feeling type who would enjoy telling you how he functions. But usually this sort of lecture does not catch the fantasy of a feeling type. He has no problem with feeling and therefore no rich fantasies about it. Whereas I would be in the same fix had I to expand upon the nature of intuitive-thinking which for me is automatic and unreflected.

So, I make the personal premise clear from the start. Learning through lectures is always a kind of distortion. Only certain sorts of people have the gift for words, so that one learns things as filtered through that sort of word-consciousness. But learning about feeling does not come primarily through reading and lectures, or even words, so these chapters are a paradox in many ways: I am not the one to teach it; it is not the best way to learn; the subject itself is perhaps beyond this sort of formulation. Still, I feel it worth trying.

CHAPTER II

Jungian Descriptions and Distinctions

I would claim for Jung that he did much for resurrecting feeling and separating it from the collective prejudices. Neither Bleuler nor Freud, the two psychological masters with whom Jung was most closely associated, clearly separated feeling from emotion, from passion, from affectivity. In psychiatric and psychoanalytic literature today the feeling function is still buried in the general category of affectivity, whereas Jung differentiated feeling as a function of consciousness equal to thinking, sensing and intuiting already in 1921 in his *Psychological Types*.

By conceptually differentiating feeling and considering it a function of consciousness, Jung made a major contribution to the history or the concept of feeling. In evaluations of Jung's typological work this achievement is often overlooked, and thereby an essential aspect of Jungian psychology is often neglected, leading to many unnecessary arguments. It is crucial to the understanding of Jungian psychology that feeling be brought to bear upon it. We cannot read Jung by intellect alone. Conscious comprehension in Jungian psychology means as well feeling comprehension. All the principal conceptual symbols (e.g., introversion, shadow, archetype, self, synchronicity) are as well experiences of feeling.

The complex may be defined most simply as a group of feeling-toned ideas; the symbol is recognized by its effect on feeling as well as by its sensuous impression, its intuitional meanings and its ideational content. Even that general goal of a Jungian analysis—the cooperative relationship between ego-consciousness and the unconscious dominants—is, as a relationship, largely a function of feeling. Jungian therapy is not, as it is sometimes mistaken to be, mainly a matter of self-*knowledge*. Self-realization is a process of feeling-realization, realizing what we feel, feeling what we are; and this process begins with the first therapeutic session, to which the person comes often owing to his disturbed feelings and which opens often with that question "How do you feel?"

The assumption of feeling had its effect also on the later developments in Jung's work, especially upon the anima concept and his explorations in many dimensions of the "feminine" pole of the psyche. The recognition of feeling can also be found in his rather free and open way of doing therapy unburdened by the rigidities of technique devised by intellect. His psychology therefore soon found ear among women and among artists, just as it soon met rejection—with notable exceptions—in those places where feeling is undervalued: contemporary scientific medicine and psychology and the academies of learning.

Jung came upon the role of feeling experimentally; his earliest descriptions of feeling stem from his association experiments, where he found pure affective reasons ("yes," "bad," "like," etc.) to stimulus words, rather than associations in the stricter sense. Already in this early work during the first decade of the century, we can trace two aspects of the concept of feeling: on the one hand, feeling as a *function* which "likes," relates, makes judgments, connects, denies, evaluates; on the other hand, feelings as *contents* (hopes, longing, angers) which act in the association experiment as factors facilitating or disturbing associations. In his first attempts (1913, 1916–17) to work out the theory of types and the concept of functions, Jung did not differentiate introversion from thinking (with its psychopathology of dementia praecox) or extraversion from feeling (with its psychopathology of hysteria). These early confusions may have been in part due to his own psychological quotient.

Before we turn to Jung's description of the feeling function, we are obliged for the sake of clarity to differentiate some of the common misconceptions about the word "feeling" itself.

First, we usually confuse feeling with *sensing*. Pain and pleasure are primarily sensations (feeling comfortable, feeling itchy, feeling exhausted). However, pain has a feeling dimension in addition to the pure sensation, inasmuch as it is bound with suffering or displeasure (*Unlust*, in the language of the German psychologists). Pleasure, too, has a feeling dimension (joy, for instance), so that we can feel disappointed or unhappy from a painful punishment or glad through a delicious dinner. Often we use the expression "I feel" when we mean more accurately "I sense." For instance, feeling cold, feeling well, feeling the satiny surface of a cloth are all primarily sensations, either sensing the internal milieu, proprioceptively, or sensing an external object. Academic psychology has tried conceptually to separate feeling and sensing in terms of internal and external. We feel subjective states and sense external objects. But Jung's use of sensation and feeling is more sophisticated: we can feel events as objective values outside in ethical actions and art objects, and so, too, we can sense inside our own subjective processes.

We also use sensing and feeling confusedly when we speak of someone as "sensitive" where we are really referring to a refine-ment of feeling, a touchiness, a quality of heightened sensibility. "Sensitives" in parapsychology refer to those with an amazing intuitive function. So, curiously, we find this mixture of terms where feeling, sensing and intuiting are indistinct. These dif-ferences cannot be made clear as the mind would like, because language follows not logical but psychological truth. Evidently the separation of functions is not sharply defined. In French, for instance, the word *sentir* (connected with our word "senti-ment") means "to feel," "to sense" and also "to foresee" (intuit). Metaphors of feeling use the language of sensation; we say "tender," "sweet," "bitter" for feelings, identifying the sensuous content of feeling with the function.

There is much justification in language for the closeness of

[handwritten marginalia at top of page:]
- feeling as a tactual connota-
tion
- feelings become affects when they
release physical innervations
(inborn) instinctual reactions

feeling and sensing. Etymologically, the root of the word "feel-ing" is *fol* (Teutonic), a cognate of *fol-m* (Anglo-Saxon), meaning palm of the hand. The same root is in the Icelandic *fal-ma* = to grope. Skeat's *Etymological Dictionary*, in fact, defines "feel" sim-ply as "to perceive by touch." From another direction there is a connection between feeling (in a broader sense) and the hand: the Greek term *orexis,* which we translate as appetite, desire and longing, means also to reach for or stretch out for, as one does with the hand. It is risky to draw big conclusions from ety-mology, but clearly feeling once had a tactual connotation.

Second, feeling is often confused with *intuiting*. Feeling cer-tain, feeling right, feeling something is rotten or fishy are all ex-pressions of intuition. We tend to say "I feel," rather than "I see" or "I find" or "It seems to me," which would be more appropriate language for stating intuitions. The statement "He has a good 'feel' for paintings" or "He can 'feel' into the back-ground of people" more likely describes intuition than feeling.

Third, feeling is often undifferentiated from *emotion, affect* and *passion* (feeling furious, excited, in love, grief). The demar-cation of the borderlines here is a major problem in psychology as I have worked out to some extent in my book *Emotion.* Jung does not generally distinguish between affect and emotion (cf. *Psychological Types, CW* 6, ¶¶ 681, 706). His distinction between feeling and emotion/affect is mainly quantitative (ibid., ¶ 681): feelings become affects when they release physical innervations. However, he does not go far enough, and an examination of the academic literature (see my *Emotion*) gives some ground for con-sidering affects as rather primordial, partial, one-sided release dynamisms, rather close to what animal behaviorists speak of with the term "inborn (instinctual) reactions," or psychiatrists with "primitive reactions." Affect lowers the mental level to what Janet has called the inferior part of a function. Emotion, on the other hand, is a total event of the personality, based perhaps in affect or having an affective component, and con-taining a feeling dimension. Many levels are activated, and consciousness becomes transformed through an emotion to a symbolic kind of consciousness. Emotions are highly significant states. They provide depth. They give and bring meaning; they disorder and create at the same time, and they present the experience of body-consciousness. In a nutshell: emotion embraces both affect and feeling and more as well; feeling is a partial activity associated with consciousness, mainly; affect is largely a physiological expression.

Fourth, feeling as a function differs from *feelings*. One can have feelings without being able to do much with them, without being able to function feelingly. (Similarly, one can have intuitions or thoughts without functioning mainly through intuition or mainly by thinking; i.e., one can have thoughts without being able to think them further to conclusions.) The feeling function may evaluate thoughts, sense-objects and psychic contents of any kind. It is not restricted to feelings. The feeling function feels (appreciates and relates to) not only feelings. We may feel our thoughts, discover their value and importance. We may feel that even the most intense sensations or grandest intuitions have little value or cannot be related to. So too, we may think feeling and about feelings—as we are doing right now in this lecture. Feelings themselves—irritation, enjoyment, boredom —may be handled adequately or inadequately, valued positively or negatively by the feeling function. We shall return to this at length in regard to "inferior functioning." So, the person who seems to have so much feeling and be so full of feelings may not be a "feeling-type" at all, whereas a feeling-type, because he disposes of feelings quite equanimously, may seem utterly devoid of feelings, distant and disinterested. Having feelings and using feeling is the difference between the contents and the process which organizes and expresses the contents. However, once this distinction is made we must not put too much weight on it. Practically, the continual subjective process of experiencing feelings is the passive background of the feeling function.

Fifth, feeling is often carelessly merged with the conceptual symbols "anima" and "Eros." Eros refers to the principle of union, attraction toward and attachment to, connection, relation, involvement which binds together. It has roots in desire and specific affects such as longing, burning, ascending, dying, and specific symbols such as wings, arrows, child, fire, ladder. As an archetypal dominant, Eros differs both from the anima as a psychological complex and from feeling as a psychological function, even if both may take on shades of Eros and come under

Eros the principle of union,
attraction towards, attachment
to
106   James Hillman

its sway in that Eros is meta-psychological, a God or Daimon, and a wider category than either anima or feeling.

Anima by definition is the feminine aspect of the masculine psyche and is always feminine. Eros, however, is masculine. Its imagery in various cultures confirms this. Kama, Eros, Cupid, Frey, Adonis, Tammuz—all are male; and the incarnations of enlightened love, Krishna, Buddha, Jesus—for all their gentleness and forbearance in regard to sexual fertility—are masculine. The eros principle is active and aimed; preaching, teaching, traveling, leading souls to redemption or heroes and men to the fateful embrace, or shooting its darts into flesh— love is male deed and power. It makes effects in the world and the psyche. Whether the movement be the homing of grace downward or the yearning upward from the imperfect to the perfect, eros remains in every context, Christian or not, a spiritual creative dynamus, a prime mover.

Although feeling can be considered to be a manifestation of eros within consciousness and the feeling function to be rooted archetypally in eros, the principle yet differs distinctly from feeling in the essential respect that feeling is human. Feeling is an individual attribute of consciousness, limited by a spatial and temporal situation. Eros is, as the writings tell us, always universal and impersonal—even inhuman and demonic. Whether as sexual compulsion or as cosmogonic eros holding the universe together, it remains impersonal, a force, not a feeling function.

Therefore, it is quite legitimate to speak of people with much eros and little feeling, or differentiated feeling and little eros. If we remember eros as a vital force that throws us into life and turmoil, messing things up, involving the psyche in matters beyond its comprehension, then we can grasp how little it has to do with a differentiated feeling function. Lovers can unite without any feeling; eros is enough to spawn all sorts of progeny, bring together all sorts of opposites into symbolic unities. On the other hand, the charming "feeler," or the introverted "deep feeler," may be far from being moved by the archetype of eros. When considering hysteria, sociopathy and schizoid withdrawal, it might be well to differentiate eros and feeling. Feeling may function quite adaptedly in the psychopathic aspect of the complex, with charm and all the manifestations of interested relatedness, yet underneath is power and self-gain, not eros. Many sins of the lack of eros are covered over by the words "introversion" or "feeling-type," so that the introverted deep-feeler may live a life where the heated confusions of eros and its aspiring dynamics never move the personality at all.

In the seminars of Jung (*Dream Analysis,* volume II, 1929/30, 3rd edition, 1958, Psychological Club Zürich, pp. 292-93)* which have not yet been authoritatively published and from which one may not quote, Jung makes some distinctions among the feeling function, love and eros. He points out that any of the functions can be under the influence of eros and not only the feeling function. Yet he does tend to consider the highest development of the feeling function to be manifested by a quality of loving. The difficulty in the distinction of these terms reflects prior difficulties within our feeling, loving and eros. Eros is a God, and having lost touch with him, we are in a mess, and we quarrel over *agape* and *philia* and *caritas* and *amicus.* No wonder: after all, who knows what love is?

The oppositions between logos and eros, between masculine and feminine, between love and power—and so many more with which we are familiar—need to be understood first of all within the *fantasy of opposites.* These are ways of making things separated, opposed and distinct; these oppositions are useful for grasping things with the mind which always needs these simplifications since it is never altogether up to the complicated nature of psychic reality, which is always complex. Thus, let us not insist so much on opposing principles, logos versus eros. There is a logos in eros as there is an eros in the spirit. These ideational principles are symbolic ideas and need to be understood each for itself in its own way and not merely as counters in a game of opposites.

The masculinity of eros must always be kept quite distinct from its feminine counterpart, with which it is usually in close association. Hence, the mythological images of Mother and Son, as aspects of each other, the son embodying and carrying into action the qualities of the mother. The great Goddess and all her

*Now published as *Dream Analysis: Notes of the Seminar Given in 1928/1930,* ed. William McGuire (Princeton: Princeton University Press, 1984).

configurations as Kuan-Yin, Devi, Ishtar, Cybele, Aphrodite, Venus, Freya, or as Maria show another quality. The essence of her love is more passive, more accepting, less differentiated. This essence, expressed negatively, is her notorious promiscuity; expressed positively, it is endless fecundity and all-embracing merciful compassion.

We cannot lose sight of the fact that any contemporary discussion of the feeling function and what it feels like will always bear the confusions of our language and our culture, where imprecise feeling and undisciplined emotion reign. Repression always has the effect of amalgamating the repressed through heat and pressure into a sticky mixture. Where the female principle, as well as feeling and eros, are repressed, women tend to be the representatives of all these virtues. But for us it is not possible to distinguish without careful analysis just what are the various properties of the amalgam. Individual analysis in psychotherapy optimistically might lead to the separation of these various virtues. Eros can then be freed from its identification with the passively feminine and indiscriminate Great Goddess; the anima-complex can be freed from its domination by eroticism; women can be relieved from the burden of carrying men's own unconscious feminine side as well as having to carry men's feeling function and their authentic and necessary commitment of eros.

Jung's definition of feeling should be read in its entirety. But we can condense from it these formulations. (See: *Psychological Types, CW* 6):

> Feeling is primarily a process that takes place between the *ego* and a given content, a process, moreover, that imparts to the content a definite *value* in the sense of acceptance or rejection ("like" or "dislike"). The process can also appear isolated, as it were, in the form of "mood," regardless of the momentary contents of consciousness or momentary sensations. (¶724)

> ... feeling is a kind of *judgment*, differing from intellectual judg-

ment in that its aim is not to establish conceptual relations but to set up a subjective criterion of acceptance or rejection. Valuation by feeling extends to *every* content of consciousness, of whatever kind it may be. When the intensity of feeling increases, it turns into an *affect,* i.e., a feeling-state accompanied by marked physical innervations. (¶725)

Feeling, like thinking, is a *rational* function, since values in general are assigned according to the laws of reason, just as concepts in general are formed according to these laws.
     Naturally the above definitions do not give the essence of feeling—they only describe it from outside. The intellect proves incapable of formulating the real nature of feeling in conceptual terms, since thinking belongs to a category incommensurable with feeling.... [Compare Mendelssohn, p. 95 above] (¶¶727–28)

When the subject's attitude as a whole is oriented by the feeling function, we speak of a *feeling type.* (¶729)

     The feeling function is that psychological process in us that evaluates. Through the feeling function we appreciate a situation, a person, an object, a moment in terms of value. A prerequisite for feeling is therefore a structure of feeling memory, a set of values, to which the event can be related. (We can see at once the importance of childhood analysis for uncovering parental influences on the structure of feeling memory and the development of values.) Some writers have stressed especially this structure of feeling memory built upon the past, and the preference of the feeling-type for past time. This rather schematic way of organizing the types according to time does have the advantage of stressing the importance of time in regard to the functions, and especially the importance of an accumulation of feeling-experiences as a basis of the feeling function. (See: H. Mann, M. Siegler, H. Osmond, "The Many Worlds of Time," *J. Analyt. Psychol.* 13: 36ff.)
     As a process that is always going on and that gives or receives feeling-tones—even the feeling-tone of indifference—this function connects both the subject to the object (by imparting value)

feeling relates subject to obj.
feeling requires more time than is needed for perception; the more differentiated the set of values the slower the process of feeling

and the object to the subject (by receiving it within the subjective value system). It therefore functions as a relation and is often called "the function of relationship." When a black cat crosses my path and I slow up, frown and sense a squirt of fear, I am relating to the event not only physiologically. The event, and the cat too, has become evaluated in terms of my subjective value system which has established positions for this situation. The feeling function has related me to this event in terms of worry and negative judgments. Events that are not evaluated but are merely perceptually recorded or entertained in the mind as fanciful intuitions have not been felt, and so I cannot be said to have any relationship with them nor they to me. I may have vivid dreams and devastating fights without feeling their value one way or another, and so they are not related to my consciousness. So, in sum, feeling relates subject to object, to the contents of one's psyche as values, and to one's subjectivity as general feeling-tone and mood.

As a process, feeling requires time, more time than is needed for perception. Like thinking, it must rationally organize perceptions and judge them; unlike thinking it judges by values. The more differentiated and rich this set of values, the slower may be the process of feeling. (Similarly with thinking, the more differentiated the ideational world, the slower may be the final placing of a new thought.) In making judgments the feeling function balances values, compares tones and qualities, weighs importance and decides upon the values it discovers. The feeling function on a more primitive level is mainly a reaction of yes and no, like and dislike, acceptance and rejection. As it develops, there forms in us a subtle appreciation of values, and even of value systems, and our judgments of feeling then rest more and more on a rational hierarchy, whether it be in the realm of aesthetic taste, ethical goods, or social forms and human relationships. Although these systems of values and the judgments coming from them are not logical, they are rational. The developed feeling function is the reason of the heart which the reason of the mind does not quite understand.

The difference between logical and rational in regard to feeling deserves perhaps more description. Although feeling does not operate in syllogisms, there is an exactitude and demon-

to thinking the more differentiated the ideational world, the slower may be the process of placing a new thought.

strable reason in its operations. For example, one develops taste, which cannot be logically explained or experimentally proved but which is yet coherent and systematic. The ability to handle a problem or talk with a person in the right way shows a rational discrimination and an adjustment to what is needed. Yet, the entire operation may not be intellectual. One says different things to different people according to the values of the situation and according to the requirements of the other person. These answers to questions may not be either truthful or correct in the logical sense, but from the point of view of feeling they may be exactly right. When a child asks for an explanation, an answer may be given from thinking or from feeling; at times, a story which answers to the anxiety in the child may be "truer" than an intellectual explanation of causes. To hit the mark truly does not mean always to tell the factual or logical truth. In therapy, a problem may often be relieved by absurdities of anecdote or parable, in the manner of the masters, rather than by relentless logical reductions. In resolving a conflict often the whole picture of harmony is more important than either logic or facts. The function of feeling then creates a situation in which viewpoints may rationally blend even though the opposing logical and factual issues have not been settled and may even have been compromised. One may be irrationally at odds with an appointment or an outer obligation, yet in tune with one's own values and mood. On waking in the morning, feeling tells us how we feel regardless of the outer rationality of weather, time on the clock, duties of the day, state of the body. And above all, feeling provides the order and logic for love.

There is a time sense connected with the feeling function which is not mentioned in the literature, yet which is part of the *ratio* of the feeling function. The sense of timing and tact is a function of feeling which is often incompatible with the reason of thinking. This division gives occasion to doing the right thing at the wrong time. There is a "feel" to each discrete moment and each chain of moments. Each life has its "feel" to it, the way its time courses, which turns a case history into a soul history, a chain of events into a patterned rhythm. A biography is the exposition of feeling running through time, the feeling of a person and a period.

Although feeling is a process of evaluation, although Jung discovered facts leading to his description of the function from evaluative statements in the association experiment, and although values are generally organized by scales, feeling cannot be simplified to fit a pain–pleasure or like–dislike system. Some theorists attempt with their logic to reduce feeling to an ultimate pair of hedonic coordinates. But the differentiation of aesthetic feeling (beautiful–ugly), of moral feeling (good–bad), of human feeling (love–hatred, elated–depressed), of biological feeling (attraction–repulsion, receding–expanding)—all point beyond mere hedonic preferences of like–dislike. Reduction of feeling to hedonic tone inevitably leads to a hedonistic philosophy in which the hierarchy of feeling values and judgments is forced into a framework of pleasure and pain. Then quantitative measures are brought in, and feeling gives way before the technical organization of thinking.

The nature of the feeling function is more complex. It does not start with simples. Like music, it starts as a *Gestalt* of melody rather than a string of primary tones. Feeling plays its tune, and a different tune in accord with each situation and with the values implicit in the situation itself. As they say in aesthetics: we judge each work of art according to the conditions it presents, the aims it itself sets out to achieve.

Even in analysis or counseling it is neither correct nor useful to attempt to discover feeling by asking, "Do you like him?", "Do you like that?" If the answer is a flat "Yes" or "No," it is usually not truly an individual feeling statement, but rather something more childish and mechanical, perhaps a family view in the sense that it is an affective reaction from the complex and not a conscious feeling judgment. Like and dislike are intricate matters, requiring weighing. The feeling answer to "Do you like him?" is "It depends." It depends: on the situation, on what I mean by "like," on what aspects of him I am asked about, and so on. The feeling function sorts all this out; it is a process, as Jung says. To reduce feeling to mere like–dislike is an intellectual devaluation; it would be similarly unjustified to reduce all thought processes to the true–false dichotomy. Reduction is anyhow a pinched way of proceeding in the psychological analysis of anything. We may separate, analyze, examine, describe; but reduction belittles because it cuts down the wholeness of an event, the existential reality of just now, what it feels like, which is always complex. This complexity is given by feeling. Feeling records the specific quality and value. And just this exploration and amplification of shadings and tones, this reversal of reduction, is a function of feeling.

We have dwelled upon these differentiations of the concept of feeling in order to demonstrate that we are not talking of feelings merely in a vague, sentimental and popular tone. It is not enough to speak of guilty feelings and hurt feelings and inadequate feelings. It is not enough to encourage people to express their feelings. Some sort of theoretical basis is also required for this word "feeling." The occupation in this chapter with the notion of feeling is part of making feeling itself more precise. It is also a way of becoming conscious of feeling, of a feeling-consciousness.

The feeling function has lain like a buried continent in the collective psyche, and it seems to be moving and causing tremors, shaking the foundations of our beliefs and values —and of course styles. All the concerns with eroticism and loneliness, with aging and delinquency, with violence and communication reflect a moment of feeling within the collective psyche. No one can escape it; everything seems so uncertain when feeling is shaken, when we can't count upon values and styles, and upon the processes of relationship that knit together the social patterns. Psychotherapy seems to have recognized this movement in the buried continent, laying its contemporary emphasis upon sensitivity, relatedness and expression of feeling. That this is a one-sided approach to the psyche, too personal and too sentimental, goes without saying. It seems that psychotherapy is rather unreflecting about the collective movements of the psyche which affect its dogmas: when sex was the great repressed, we had the Viennese influence; then it was the mother-complex everywhere, nourishing and breasts; now, it is a matter of the feeling function; soon, aggression, violence and enmity will be the theme.

At the moment, as I revise these lectures (1970), feeling has become the content and procedure of therapy. We are in a new Romantic age where feeling is all; we have become feeling-addicts—"How does it feel," "Express your feelings," "What do you feel about it." Communication has become centered upon the description of feelings, replacing the communication of ideas and insights. Moreover, the intellectual spirit of the psyche and the communication of thought are regarded as a betrayal of the "movement" and of what is "human" and being a "real person." Again we see how thinking and feeling fall into archaic oppositions. And these feelings, expressed and shared in therapeutic groups and the new sorts of communities, are so incredibly personal and boring! We are so fond of believing that what is most personal is also most individual, but the personal, including the ego, reflects commonplaces and generalities. The intimate adventures of one's feeling "trips," like the home-movies of the trip through the national parks, are boring because the psyche gets no food from only the personal. Experience must be turned into something fantastic to hit the psyche; that is, it needs to take on a poetic, metaphoric, mythic aspect that goes beyond what one personally felt. There is a false assumption in the new therapy cults which emphasize personal feeling. An opposition is made between personal experience and general or impersonal or abstract experience. But the personal is only one level of general, common experience. Everyone feels afraid under attack, longs for what he doesn't quite know, quarrels, hates and back-bites. The personal might better be viewed as feeling on the banal level of the ego, myself the sincere adolescent as sensitive center of the universe.

It is indeed pathetic to realize how estranged from feeling and its forms we have become so that we must play in sand-boxes, crawl on the floor, run naked in the woods, have strangers put their hands on us, or have professional practitioners read cheap poetry so that we might "feel something." Yet, always behind all immediate trends is the psyche itself struggling with soul-making, now in terms of feeling. This lost and degenerated function shows itself in awkward tenderness and sensitivity, in attempts to touch, to reach out, to encounter— only to be systematized by the therapists into profitable professional schemes for teaching how to be sensitive, to touch and to encounter. Maybe these new programs have more value than my feeling credits them with. But there are other ways of feeling, as these lectures hope to show.

CHAPTER III

Feeling-Types

In actuality the types are not easily recognized. The functional type is rarely evident, for as Anaximander said, and the Buddha too: whatever exists is a mixture of many elements; whatever exists is impure. There are no pure types; there are no people in whom only one function operates and nothing else. But there are those in whom the overall "attitude of the individual is oriented by the function of feeling," and, following Jung, these we call feeling-types.

Jung's description covers thoroughly what he meant by introverted and extraverted feeling-types; these descriptions have been expanded by many Jungian writers since. Rather than go over the ground again, it might be useful to expose some clichés about feeling-types because these notions, conceived in jargon, work to the detriment of feeling and maintain its undervaluation. Some of these clichés, for instance, hold that musicians are "feelers," or that people who have "good eros" are feeling-types, or that women, just because they are women, have better access to feeling.

Let us take these notions one by one. The relationship of

music and feeling has never been carefully worked out. Whether in composition or execution, its range is not limited by one type of person. That it is not verbal does not necessarily mean that music does not have intellectual content or require thinking. Like any art form, music unites opposites in itself and is not the privilege of a special psychological function, unless that function be called "musical talent." Music hath charms to tame the savage beast, and Orpheus enchanted *all* the animals with his lyre. So, when we listen feelings are stirred, but this again does not mean that we use especially the feeling function to listen to music nor that the feeling-type listens most accurately.

Furthermore, there is a curious Apollonic aspect of music that can lead consciousness into inhuman strata, cold, distant, cruel even. The relationship of music and the military deserves much more examination: Achilles, the greatest slayer in the *Iliad,* had a special relation to music; Apollo committed his worst crime (against Marsyas) for music; and Nazi generals and concentration camp commanders enjoyed beautiful concerts. We tend to sentimentalize both music and the feeling function, missing that each can have a psychopathic aspect.

Next let us stress again the difference between eros as an archetypal principle and feeling as a function. They are quite distinct. For example: some people may have taste, sensitive differentiated feeling with cultural depth, yet be crooks, or be wholly auto-erotic, without a touch of eros in the sense of burning involvement, care and love. Or the reverse: one may be all eros, almost a mythical lover, outpouring and compassionate and yet be wholly out of touch with one's subjective sense of feeling values and the outer objects, causes and people to whom one is devoting one's life. A woman may love and wait for a worthless drunkard who is in prison for crimes. Her feeling may have no discrimination and be in a mess, but her eros is there. Or, take a look at people in love: they are swimming in eros, and at the same time they may be lying and cheating and cruelly hurting each other and society. But then people in love may not be a good example for either eros or for feeling!

Another source of clichés about feeling concerns the role of women. Women have been burdened with the distaff side of the masculine psyche. Men presume that what they have not got, women have. Where men have failed to become conscious of their own feeling function, they take over from women feeling judgments and values and establish patterns of relationship which are not their own. This illusion is perpetuated every time a woman takes her husband by the hand to a concert, a cathedral, or a clothing store. Here, her feeling function is supposed to be educating her husband's culture and taste. Masculine patterns of relationship—as, for instance, between friends and enemies, military, laboratory, business organizations, the conduct of the law, parliament and clubs and unions—are activities and places of the feeling function of men, so that the feeling function need not be identified with women and pushed on to them. When Jung in his description of the types declares that feeling-types are found more often among women, his statement may be taken as an observation of our society, but not as a psychological law. It is in fact one of the insidious clichés of our time (and one which Jungian psychology has not done enough to dispel) that eros and feeling have an affinity with women. In this model the feeling of men can never be rightly understood, so that friendship feelings get called latent homosexuality or transference. In a society where men must look to women for their feeling education (moral and aesthetic values, organization of relationships, manners and style, expression of feelings), the male feeling type will go around in disguise and will not even be recognized by his own psychological kin, who also wear masks of "good feeling" designed by women. Often a man comes into his own feeling function when with other men (e.g., military service, at the office, or in an adulterous love affair where its course and rhythm depend upon his feeling lead).

Another usual view is that warmth, gaiety and enthusiasm are the same as feeling, and that feeling-types can be recognized by their outgoing relatedness. However, an intuitive person, or somebody who has not quite grown up, or a hysterical person can also display these same, sometimes charming, virtues and yet have misplaced and inappropriate feeling. The uninhibited bring to a situation a free flow of feelings; this is not to say that they bring as well a differentiated feeling function. It is also claimed that people who are cold are not feeling-types. Nevertheless, feeling can be expressed in cold, exact, remote manners, as in diplomatic language and in realms of aesthetic taste where classical formulations and accuracy can be compared with the exquisiteness of mathematical formulae.

Sometimes we forget that the application of law by a judge is an operation of feeling, and that laws were invented not merely to protect property or assure the priesthood and ruling-class of their power, but also to evaluate difficult human problems and to do justice in human affairs. Judging is a matter of feeling, just as in the temples of Saturn a balance was displayed, or as Saturn in a horoscope is said to be well-placed when in the sign of Libra. A Solomonic decision is not one brilliant stroke through the Gordian knot of complexities, but rather a judgment made by feeling. Law concerns "cases," considers "claims" and "obligations," and by means of it one can make "appeals." The Bill of Rights is a document of the feeling function at its abstract best. We erroneously believe that feeling must always be personal and that law is always cut and dried, forgetting the impersonal feeling values of law, of its ideals and its general application.

In his *Education through Art* (London, 1943), Herbert Read develops the eight types into connections with styles of painting. He believes that extraverted feeling tends toward decorative art and introverted feeling toward imaginative art. Here again is the beginning of a cliché about feeling: extraverted feeling is "only" descriptive, superficial, a play of color and forms, without deep content, as compared with introverted feeling with its access to the creative imagination. Here, we tend to miss that imagination, because it is archetypally governed, can produce stereotypes, and, on the other hand, decoration can elaborate marvelous patterns from the most archaic basket and pottery designs to the intricacies of Islamic stonecarving. Subtlety and intricacy can be virtues of extraverted feeling which have no less value because they do not come on "deep" and "strong."

Another pet notion about feeling-types is that wherever they are present an atmosphere of good feeling prevails. Feeling-types, however, by their insistence upon values, and the structures in which these values are embedded, may often be highly intolerant of deviations or of values which are new. Feeling-types take time, so that often they inhibit movement with their slowness because they tune into an atmosphere. If it is not to their suiting, they subtly impose their feeling world or disturb the one taking place by undercutting it. If they do not like the atmosphere and cannot change it, they may spend the evening in silence, unable to take part at all, meanwhile passing silent judgments, or attempting, if extraverted, to turn things into adapted sociable channels. The importance of ideas, the beauty of wild intuitions, or sensations just as they are, are not enough. Things must be evaluated and related to.

Then, too, they have difficulty with the irrational, since feeling is a rational function, perhaps not logical yet always reasonable. The irrational types find themselves hamstrung and irritated by the feeling-types' disinterest with, and even sabotage of, "crazy" things, people, events. They have a good hand which smooths and straightens—and which also smothers. They do not like conflict, preferring to balance extremes, not by taking the opposite extreme, but through deflating extremity as such, making it seem ridiculous, disproportionate. They say "don't get so worked up" or "it's not all that important" or "wait 'til tomorrow." Or, where things are "crazy" and out of hand, they find ways again to make it palatable, either with a little joke that takes the edge off, or by evaluating it with a positive judgment, like "it's probably better this way" or "it seems mad, but it's really a good thing." These oiling and diplomatic methods help civilize life, but for the sake of this "good feeling" change is often blocked. Even in close relationships, feeling-types seem to have an eye for the soft spot in the other and can put the needle in. They can masterfully handle those places in a relationship which the non-feeling-type painfully tries to cover and does not wish exposed. Sometimes in discussions they put in the needle not personally, but by making the theme of the discussion banal or by killing it with an archaic and collective doubt from their inferior thinking.

In relationships feelers need to be in touch with the other person's feelings. Other types can carry on for hours without awareness that the person with whom they are talking is not there with his feelings, or is even hostile. Sometimes other types do not know even to whom they are pouring out their hearts and dearest ideas. But feelers must have this contact, or they lose "touch" and go "off." They have a bad evening or a bad hour of analysis. The analyst who is not a feeler warms to his theme, gets interested in the "material," and never notices that the feeling-type analysand is only interested in the feeling thing going on between them. For the analyst (a non-feeler, in this example) all his feeling is in the work; but the analysand feels cut off from himself by being cut off from the feeling. By losing touch with his first function he feels rejected, and then he concludes erroneously about himself and the situation, because the complexes have taken over or he becomes a victim of inferior thinking, delusions and negative ideas.

This penchant of the feeling-type for maintaining touch with the other's feeling function is not merely making everything "personal" as he is often accused of; it is truly of importance for the feeling function itself to keep a stream of relating between subject and events. This is how it functions, its *raison d'être*. A feeler usually does not follow the flow of thought in a discussion, although he may be attentively evaluating the thought. At the films he does not have to follow the plot in order to "get" the picture, since he learns as much from the actors, the aesthetic values or ethical content, or the import of the content for his own life. For an event not to be a waste, it must provide the feeler with opportunity for the function to exercise itself; otherwise he is deprived of his way of being-in-the-world and feels out of sorts.

The necessity to evaluate can be quite a bore for non-feeling types. A feeler never seems able to just perceive and observe; he must pass judgments and thereby bring himself into relationship with the events he has evaluated. A feeling-type must describe the tenant upstairs as "that nice lady on the fifth floor," or "the nasty little night-watchman," "that peculiar analyst," etc. His descriptions are loaded with adjectival commentary which says "like" or "dislike," "good" or "bad." But that tenant on the fifth floor is neither horrid nor ugly, nor nice, nor officious —or, rather, she is *all* of these things and much more. By passing judgment, feeling puts things into place, and then they do not need to be looked at again. In this way feeling-types put a stop to discussion, because they stop further psychological observation. Once they are done with the evaluative process, the issue is rather closed. Sometimes, because of their fixed positions, feeling-types seem unintelligent, whereas it is actually their inflexibility about the values assigned. The feeling-type is loyal to his feeling process and to its results in judgments and to the relationships made. But, by passing judgment and making relations, he brings to a halt the flow of observations and perceptions of the irrational functions. Feeling-types do not change their views; they make loyal friends and put up with all sorts of faults, for they have already taken their stand, so that the person to whom they have given friendship is no longer in question. Thus, they do indeed tend toward conservatism, as has been brought out in the paper by Mann, Siegler and Osmond mentioned above.

Another cliché concerns the sincerity and straightness of feeling-types. People without good feeling, it is said, cannot be trusted; their values are off; they betray; they waver. Feeling-types, it is believed on the other hand, are expert at relationship and can lead feeling into positive channels in others. However, differentiated feeling of the feeling-type can get away with anything and can be just the reverse of honesty and straightforwardness. Moreover, feeling-types do not necessarily lead anything out of others. By aiming to keep an aura of good feeling, they may encourage everything and dampen everything, indiscriminately soothing away worry, making spiritual concerns "not really so important," flattening panics and hysterics, all of which nips in the bud the libidinal content that is trying to emerge by means of the excitement.

We must recognize that "being human" is not only a matter of human feeling, but of human ideas and spirit. When feeling-types are threatened by ideas, unable to relate to them or see their significance *as ideas,* they act as anti-spirits, as *Ungeist,* and put down an essence of what is human in the name of feeling. For it is just as important to think and reflect and intuit and perceive as it is to feel; not only feeling makes for what is "human."

One further idea about feeling we might well question. We are used to conceiving the types as *either* extraverted *or* introverted. We place the function within the fantasy of opposites.

being human not only human
feeling but also ideas
& spirit

But suppose prior to these opposites, there is the single function of feeling not divided into two kinds of feeling. Suppose there is always some introverted and some extraverted feeling going on whenever the function is in use. In other words, perhaps the function is never altogether moving one way, but has a certain ambivalence about it.

At a party or when having to perform in public we very often experience feeling on two levels at once: engagement and reserve, for instance. To call one aspect of this ambivalence "schizoid" or mark it off to a shadow or an anima/-us does not do the actual experience justice. Why should we be "whole-hearted" any more than "singleminded"? In highly charged situations, two sides of feeling often appear together showing an archetypal level of the feeling function: grief and laughter, desire and disgust, love and aggression often combine within the same intense relationship at the very same moment. Why not the introverted and extraverted aspects too? Cannot a function introvert and extravert at the same time? Can I not observe and reflect simultaneously?

In a differentiated feeling-type the two sides of his function work harmoniously. I believe that the supposed "coldness" of the feeling-type may be accounted for by this harmony between his outer related rapport with the objective situation and his inner subjective values. The coldness is merely the mastery of a tension which would make most of us hot under the collar. We would have to sacrifice adaptation to be "true" to what we feel or compromise our values to conform. But not the differentiated feeling-type! He can "get away with murder" through excellent adaptation yet not lie to himself since the introverted aspect of the function maintains him in rapport with his values. Another type where the function is only one-sided (introverted *or* extraverted) would have a moral crisis and play the matter up into existential dimensions of honor, sincerity, truth and so on. The feeler simply digests inwardly the outer aspect of his actions, their necessity and appropriateness within the context, and according to his main value: maintenance of flowing connections.

Extraverted feeling ought not be confused with the persona. Although in Jung both refer to the process of adaptation, extraverted feeling is a function of personality. It is a manner of performing and can be an expression of an individual style. By means of it a person gives values and adapts to values in ways which can be highly differentiated, uncollective and original. The persona, on the other hand, is a fundamental archetype of the psyche referring to the manner in which consciousness reflects with society. The persona in Jung's stricter usage of the term, therefore, does not refer to something individual. A developed persona would mean a developed reflection of the collective consensus. If one is a prisoner, or an addict, or a hermit, or a general, one can have a developed persona by behaving in the styles and forms collectively belonging to these patterns of existence. They are archetypal patterns. Feeling may have little or nothing to do with this adaptation, for one can be connected very well to the collective through thinking, intuition and sensation. In a nutshell: classically, the persona is a collective way of playing a role in the world; the feeling function is an individual instrument of self-affirmation.

In all, the feeling-type is generally oriented by the feeling function, which means that he steers his life according to feeling values and the processes in relationship. To go beyond this simple statement would be to fall again under the influence of the clichés that feeling-types (a) have more feelings, or (b) have special kinds of feelings, or (c) have only good or superior feelings.

A convenient, rule-of-thumb way of distinguishing the feeling-type is through its opposite. Recalling with Moses Mendelssohn that we cannot feel and think at the same time and with Jung that feeling and thinking are incompatible, we would expect people who habitually feel themselves through life to have difficulties with thinking and with thoughts. If to feel competently means to think poorly, then we would expect to find feeling-types nervous about ideas.

Feeling-types tend to become fantastic and emotional in thought, but the thought itself, so overwhelmingly important, cannot be thought further, cannot be carefully worked out. It remains doctrinaire. Rather than their having ideas, ideas seem to have them. Frequently, they read too much and indiscriminately or they do not read at all. The all-or-none reaction is common in other realms where thinking shows itself; for instance, thoughtful planning becomes either over-exact or carelessly magical. Feeling-types may well devote themselves to an idea, but this ideational program will often turn out to be strange, archaic, crack-pot. Sometimes the thoughts they think at sixty have all the pristine splendor they had when they first entered their minds in college. So they find themselves imprisoned by old narrow views and become rigid in their thinking rather than either serious or playful. Even the ideas they have about themselves may suffer in this manner, so that what they are and what they think they are in no way tally. The inferior thinking only perpetuates conditions that no longer exist and furthers a neurosis by keeping an inflexible frame on a personality that has long since outgrown it. They may be prey to weird speculative worries about logical and metaphysical problems such as the nature of truth and the end of the world. The attic of their minds stored with antique furniture may nevertheless become a lumber room for creative work, in that the unknown inferior parts of the psyche contain the stuff of originality.

CHAPTER IV

Inferior Feeling and Negative Feelings

The inferior thinking function of the feeling-type allows characterization, even caricature, whereas the description of inferior feeling, because it is a general cultural problem and therefore has historical and collective aspects, leads into deeper waters. Inferior feeling embraces the problems of our day, and the rest of this chapter—even the rest of these lectures—will be attempts to come to terms with this inferiority which we all share.

One or two distinctions are necessary before proceeding further. First, having feelings and using the feeling function are not the same thing; therefore, having inferior feelings and using the feeling function in an inferior way are also not to be identified. This leads to a second distinction: positive and negative feelings as *contents* differ from superior and inferior *use* of the feeling function. I may well have positive feelings of love and awe for you and be so inferior in my feeling function that I have no way of expressing these feelings except through some blurted gaucherie, embarrassing to us both. On the other hand, I may feel hurt and resentful and be able to handle these feelings directly with you so adequately that they can be brought into our relationship and aid its continuity. Feelings as contents of the psyche may carry plus or minus signs. They may be negatively inferior in various senses of negative, i.e., regressive remnants from childhood, socially condemned, morally evil, or perhaps humanly destructive. But these feelings are not the feeling function, which can only be said to be inferior when it functions in a distorted, inappropriate and inadequate way. A mark of a superior feeling function, on the other hand, is the adequate handling of negative and inferior feelings. To keep these distinctions better in mind let us refer to feelings as either positive or negative (even if the plus or minus sign be usually a cultural variable) and to the use of the feeling function as either superior or inferior.

The distinction between inferior and negative comes out clearly in our relationship to children. Distorted, inadequate expression of the inferior feeling function—sexualized taste, sugary hypocrisy, faint praise, loud uncertainty, cruel correction —from the side of the parents does more damage than the direct expression of negative feelings: anger, dislike, panic, etc.

To make the difference yet clearer, let us keep trying to separate once again feelings from the feeling function. Feelings may be pleasant and unpleasant, constructive and destructive, outgoing and withholding. All of these feelings, tones and moods belong to the human gamut. They may be cruel and vicious and socially unacceptable, but their existence within the psyche is part of our nature. They are potentialities of the personality; human history shows an unbelievable range of possible feelings. Their justification is simply their existence as part of the flora and fauna of the psychic world. Our difficulties concern those feelings in this jungle to which we attach a negative sign. These are the feelings we wish to "get rid of" or "find some place for," and which usually appear unwantedly in moments when the ego loses its suppressive ability.

Depression is one such example of negative feeling, that is, a feeling judged negative by the feeling function, either because we do not like its tone, or because we do not feel its value, or because it is not approved by the value system of the culture. But is depression "negative"? Psychotherapy has surely taught us all the signal importance of going down through depressions

so that they become re-valued. When we speak of the development of feeling two things are meant. First, the admission into
consciousness of whatever feelings actually are happening—
even if they carry a minus sign—so that they are no longer repressed. Admission into the light of consciousness provides
them with a modicum of awareness and control. They are then
known, even accepted as part of its tone and content. They then
begin to qualify consciousness. In this way an integration takes
place by means of the feeling function between the conscious
personality and the negative feeling. The ego gives its personal
stamp to the feelings while the feelings alter the ego's conventional stand.

Second, the development of feeling means an evolution of
the function away from its narrowly subjective base toward a
freer adaptation. It is the over-subjectivity that leads to the
intensity of feeling-life and the inadequacy of expression. Even
feelings with a positive sign, such as love and joy, can be handled inferiorly, expressed in the wrong way at the wrong time.
An inferior function therefore helps to maintain a deposit of
"negative" feelings or even to create them with its misjudg-
ments. Let us bear in mind that any feeling can become negative
when it is mishandled. Even the most pleasant and approved
ones of altruistic love and religious worship can be loaded with
delusional intensity and over-subjectivity. So, too, any feeling
—even the most peculiar and condemned, like betrayal and
sadism—can become sources of insight and appropriate behavior in the hands of a superior feeling function.

When we give inadequate feeling to our feeling contents, they
take on distorted value, and then this distortion is what we offer
the world and its situations. We pass on judgments and values
which we have not digested. Not the feelings, but the inferiority
of our functioning makes us spoil our joys and hurt the ones we
love. In keeping distinct "negative" and "inferior" we do well to
observe: (a) that every feeling has the right to exist and its appropriate place and (b) that the feeling function can be trusted
to find eventually this appropriate place and adequate form.

For example, *nostalgic longings* return again and again whenever the ego lets down its guard, in drowsiness, in drink, when

assailed by a smell. Once we accept them, we discover that these longings refer not only to what one once had and wants to have again. They tell us that at this moment we are incomplete. This lack of fullness is inadequately expressed, not by the longings themselves, without which we would feel no lack, but by the memory images to which the longings have grown attached owing to their suppression. When I begin to feel that I long, I can begin to discover for what I actually long, and then some movement toward reflection and, even perhaps, fulfillment can be initiated. Or, as another example, musical sentimentality of trashy tunes and kitschy words is not only vulgar feeling. When stood for as what and where one actually feels, this sentimentality spread the world over by a million violins or boys' voices and guitars becomes my personal taste rather than just the world's lament wailing through me. Through affirmations of this sort we encourage the feeling function to trust its values and judgments. It can then move on from its simpler preferences and obsessive moods. As with thinking: a child does not spend all its years doing sums; soon it wants more complicated operations than addition. By giving negative feelings a chance to have their say, they either develop into appropriate hatreds and uglinesses, discriminating real values where hatred and ugliness belong, or they become boring and fall away.

Especially important for the development of feeling are just these negative feelings, these with the minus sign: envy, hatred, arrogance, complaint, etc. They in particular demand courage and honesty, requiring patience in their handling. Relating them appropriately to the contents of consciousness and relating with them adequately in situations which call for them are certainly signs of superior feeling. For this reason the enemy is important, and for this reason the negative aspects of relationships are such an essential part of life. Deeper connections offer an opportunity for negative feelings, whereas the usual place —the family—in which they are usually just spilled out is only poisoned by them. However, the negative feelings of someone with an inferior feeling function are usually so repressed and therefore so charged that they are no longer feelings but affects. It is enough here to emphasize that the education of negative feeling does *not* mean the education of it away from negativity toward its opposite, by turning all dislikes into likes, by convert ing all enemies into friends.

An early sign of inferior feeling is loss of contact with what one feels. The stuff and substance of the feeling function are usually feelings (not that the feeling function does not also evaluate thoughts and sensations as well). But when the feeling function is inferior and goes underground, as it were, with it goes an orienting awareness of how I feel, what I want, whom I like, etc., all of which is replaced by a general dryness in regard to myself and others, followed by indiscriminate complex-reactions: all sorts of displaced feelings, tears at the wrong time, wry jokes, peculiar attachments and enthusiasms, value-judgments creeping in where irrelevant, or general undifferen tiated mood swings of general elation or general depression.

The effort of maintaining consciousness with a function which is not primary is often too demanding. The function seems to come and go, not a useful tool at the regular disposal of my needs and intentions. An inferior function requires a disproportionate amount of energy: it is quite extraordinary, for instance, how much time an introverted sensation-type can spend upon fantasies of the future, upon negative paranoid in tuitions. Or, watch how much energy a relationship consumes when either of the people insists upon the personal feeling level and at the same time either or both of the partners have inferior feeling. Marriage often reflects this state: endless discussions, endless investment in feeling, because the function does not just function by itself. Then, instead of feeling, there are feelings: resentments, needs, desires, complaints.

One can notice the feeling function slip away from con sciousness. Suddenly, one feels nothing or a wave of negative feelings surges which cannot be handled adequately, resulting in anxiety and guilt. One is talking, and suddenly one's own voice begins to sound back in one's ears: the other person has become bored, the relationship loses interest, the words spoken are no longer carrying importance. Alfred North Whitehead (*Modes of Thought*) made a great deal of the word "importance" in his philosophy: it refers to the feeling aspect. The feeling function can give importance to matters beyond their matter-of-fact significance, and inferior feeling can deprive significant matters of their importance or blow up matters of insignificance into grand dimensions of importance. Demagogues have this ability of giving importance to insignificant issues through the use of feeling.

Inferior feeling puts the wrong values on things; its main disaster is in its introverted aspect when it gives the wrong feeling to oneself. Then one's judgment about oneself is distorted and inadequate. One feels inferior owing entirely to an inferior feeling function. Re-establishing the connection to oneself often requires renewed contact with the complexes through dreams or with the immediate circle of friends, family and colleagues where feeling is usually less taxingly expressed. But when the function is inferior, one feels cut off. Dreams are felt as enemies; the immediate circle is experienced only as a demand. The lost feeling function gets projected: "everyone expects feeling from me."

To feel one's worth is no easy matter. Patients expect assurance from their analysts; analysts expect confirmation from their patients. We lose touch with the importance of ourselves, alternating between depressive worthlessness and delusions of grandeur. We demand too much on the one hand and sell ourselves cheap on the other; self-confidence is shaky. When we meet with defeat, inferior feeling cannot discriminate and particularize the specific area of inferiority, but generalizes it into a devastating sense of worthlessness. We don't miss just one step, but fall down the entire flight. One faux pas, one failure, one messed-up encounter is just what it is. It is not an existential debacle which means one has lost everything or that one is no good at all. The task is to learn the algebra or to apologize for the insult, not to go off somberly and walk the streets all night examining one's character and destiny. Feeling can function as a guard or filter to prevent these archetypal levels of disaster from shattering the whole personality. Feeling is classically spoken of as the "humanizing" function, as if through feeling one became "human." This is of course a confused and sentimental notion, but it does state in its own way that feeling can differentiate between that which is authentically a fault and personal blame, and the archetypal level

of despair with its profound sense of sin, misery and empti-
ness.

This brings us to guilt. When there are more feelings than the
function can manage, there is an internal guilt toward one's
feelings. We owe something; they have not been sorted out,
made aware, declared. Here again a cultural attitude interferes
because we are not "supposed" to present some "negative" feelings (how envious and ambitious we feel, how rude we might
like to be, how fallen and despairing it seems). In the new encounter groups where the presentation of negative feelings is de
rigueur, again guilt constellates, now for other reasons. Guilty
feelings can't be shed over a weekend. Communication and expression are only one-half of feeling. There are secrets that must
be kept for the sake of individuality; there are sacrednesses.
Moreover, an attempt to do away with guilt neglects its reality,
that it is a fundamental and existential component of our Western human nature. The guilt we have got rid of only returns as a
guilt toward the guilt. Freud understood its reality and en-
shrined guilt as the super-ego. Curiously, though, guilt supports
the ego; it makes us feel that what has happened is "mine," my
fault to be set right by "me." Things that go wrong are not allowed by guilt to be left on that level of bad or unfortuitous happenings; they become problems for the ego to amend. In this
way guilt serves the ego and strengthens its hold, even allowing
the ego to extend its range over happenings by feeling itself
"responsible." But the Gods are responsible, and we are responsible to them, not to and for events. The actual fault for which
one "feels guilty" may lie in the inferiority of the feeling function, so that guilty feelings are signals of inadequacy and inap-
propriateness. Again the guilt is partly toward the function, not
giving it its exercise, rather than only to the events which seem
to cause the guilt. Ultimately, our guilt is toward the Gods, and it
is this archetypal perspective which could be seen as the true
purpose of guilt: to remind us through the feeling function of
our neglect of the Gods.

Family guilt toward one's children—that one did not do right
by them and love them—or toward the parents for the same
reasons are a guilt imposed by feeling. This guilt says that there

are feeling laws to be observed, that relationships are not merely human and personal, that there are archetypal principles of feeling which require obeisance. Feeling itself is owed something. We may well feel guilt, we believe, *because* of the complexes, for the faults they produce in our behavior; yet there is also a guilt—if not the very same one—*to* the complexes. Our responsibility is primarily to them. Guilty feelings can be turned back upon themselves by insighting them for what is owed to the complex, the care and awareness of one's specific kinds of inadequacy. Because guilt makes everything so personal, we lose the sense of impersonal guilt. I owe not only my personal feelings something, but there is an impersonal guilt toward feeling and values in general as well. The less this is recognized, the more it presses into personal affairs: so the accumulated guilts toward the body and the Dionysian and the feminine and the dark and their associated depressive feelings become personal guilt toward the oppressed people and the weak, and this guilt then appears in personal relationships with the underprivileged, the black and the physical. The guilty party is the function itself, guilty for not performing its function, since an activity not used is guilty of its inactivity. The load of guilty feelings we carry in our culture is not merely a super-ego of a Protestant ethic; there is a profound guilt toward feeling, of feeling, within feeling.

Another habit of inferior feeling is its para-psychological appearance. Where feeling has an intuitive admixture and is radically dissociated from consciousness, which is often the case in mediums and others with a para-psychological gift, connections may be maintained, not via conscious relating and human interest in the other, but via the unconscious in uncanny synchronistic events, or through dreams and prayers. These events call up the strong emotions of mystical belief. One believes in a fateful connection, in a relationship transcending space and time, in two hearts that beat as one. Despite this occult beauty, the simple human communication is failing and is replaced with wonders and witchery. Sometimes a telephone call is more human and effective than intercessory prayer. Telepathic communication means simply feeling (*pathos*) at a long distance (*tele*). ESP can be seen as an activity of the feeling function when that function has let go the threads of direct communication. When the psychological distance between people is too great, when they are humanly remote from each other, then as a substitute for this distorted relationship inferior feeling oper-ates autonomously through ESP events. Synchronicity, dreaming of each other, queer occurrences may become dodges, covering up the painful challenges of human decency.

Should intuition be an inferior function and be blurred with feeling, then perceptions about people become hyper-personal and evaluative. Intuition alone, like sensation, simply reports discrete observations, enjoying the faculty of perception, noting events and playing with their possibilities and meanings. But feeling does not let perceptions alone; what are simply facts and observations to the perceptive functions—which neither judge, nor value, nor even link perceptions into an order—inferior feeling must organize into vices and virtues. Feeling-intuition is never satisfied to see only; it must connect as well. When these functions are inferior, one sees in the light of wrong values and relates from the standpoint of false perceptions. A good deal of what we call paranoid happens in this way. We attribute nasty motives and bad values very personally to others, having gathered these feelings only from suspicions and hunches. Such wrong perceptions and evaluations are not only projections "to be taken back," but are manifestations of feeling, attempting to comprehend and evaluate a world where it is partly blind and halt.

Inferior feeling has trouble standing for its feelings. It has trouble supporting its own principles and values, especially if it has to take on an unpleasant task or hurt someone. A man may rule an organization yet be unable to fire an inefficient or disloyal secretary; the parent in the family who takes over the punishing of the children will usually be the one with the better feeling function; an analyst with inferior feeling will be unable to cope with his and the analysand's aggression.

When it does have a principle to defend, inferior feeling may of course overdo it. In women the animus comes in to help overdo things. A woman breaks with her lover and makes the

cut surgically or like an architect according to plan. Her values
are iron-clad, and she finds a lawyer to support them! Should
the man or husband want to see her again, she will be
unyielding in finding "no reason" for meeting. It just drags
things out; it's only his anima-pathos. The reason to see him
may be feeling itself, but inferior feeling does not evaluate
itself; its energy is on its evaluations, formulations of feeling, affects, and the all-or-none reaction of "in-love" or "cut-off."

When there are ingredients of sensation in the inferior feeling, then the sensuous content of feeling, its physical component, becomes confused with the evaluative process. Then we
simply cannot distinguish feeling sad and low from physical ill
health, or we confirm a happy marriage in terms of sexual inter-
course, although marriages and love relationships often exist
with little sensuous content, where sensation does not have to
carry feeling. Feeling can be expressed in highly abstract forms,
and relationships can proceed during separations.

Inferior feeling, to sum it up, may be characterized by con-
tamination with the repressed which tends to manifest, as the
Scholastic would have said, in *ira* and *cupiditas*. Inferior feeling
is loaded with anger and rage and ambition and aggression as
well as with greed and desire. Here we find ourselves with huge
claims for love, with massive needs for recognition, and discover our feeling connection to life to be one vast expectation
composed of thousands of tiny angry resentments. This expectation has been called an omnipotence fantasy, the expression of
the abandoned child with his left-over feelings that nobody
wants to take care of—but is this enough? Omnipotence is more
than a content; rather it expresses, as does the child, an impoverished functioning that insists upon more sway and exercise. Without this exercise, feeling turns upon itself, morbidly;
we are envious, jealous, depressed, feeding on needs and their
immediate gratification, then rushing out intermittently to
meet someone to help or for help. The cat neglected becomes
the unconscious tiger.

Differentiated feeling is the cat, moving in small ways.
Perhaps, feeling can be defined as the art of the small—the
shade of difference, the subtle emphasis, the little touch. It can

watch a relationship unfold, gardening it along, husbanding the forces. One can separate between needing and demanding, between what one likes and what one wants; one can shop without buying. Or the reverse: one can at last buy without shopping because one knows what one feels. One can appreciate and act without the personal erotic connection upon which so much feeling falsely and laboriously depends, with its chant: "make it mine, make it mine."

CHAPTER V

Feeling and the Mother-Complex

The difficulty we have in recognizing the feeling-type can partly be blamed on the fact that all that passes for feeling is not an expression of the feeling function. These feeling substitutes and feeling distortions arise in general from the "feminine" side of the psyche. Femininity and feeling are believed to belong together. Sometimes we say that feeling is "feminine" and to be "feminine" is to feel. Without subscribing to this, one must still recognize that in our civilization, whatever the account, feeling is placed in the hands of the feminine to mold, so that it is over-determined by women. First of all mothers, and next sisters and aunts, grandmothers and teachers, and then childhood lovers exert their influence over the development of the feeling function in men and women. The values of social behavior and the judgments formed, from etiquette to evil, all the "whats" and "hows" we should feel are given by women, from the dancing-coach and decorator to the waitress and salesgirl. The feeling function has become Whistler's "Mother," a little old lady of sweet admonitions, and we have got these kindly counsels of hers mixed with the voice of nature so that the Little Old Lady

sometimes substitutes for the Wise Old Man. Comforting
clichés about "life" and "how it goes" replace perceptive wisdom. The psychotherapist, rough and tweedy, bearded and
pipe-smoking, may then have nothing more to say than a pro-
verb from a Christmas calendar because his warmth and good
grey "wisdom" are collective enactments of the "good feeling"
the mother-complex expects from every good Dad. It is not
therefore astonishing to find the mother-complex and the
anima-complex responsible throughout life for many disorders
in the feeling function.

The mother-complex is basic to our most permanent and in-
tractable feelings. In this sense the mother is, as Jung said, fate.
This complex is the permanent trap of one's reactions and
values from earliest infancy, the box and walls in every situation
whichever way one turns. One faces the mother, as fate, ever
again and anew. Not only the contents of feelings, but the function itself takes patterns from the reactions and values which
come to life in the mother-child relationship. The way we feel
about our bodily life, our physical self-regard and confidence,
the subjective tone with which we take in or go out into the
world, the basic fears and guilts, how we enter into love and
behave in closeness and nearness, our psychological temper-
ature of coldness and warmth, how we feel when we are ill, our
manners, taste, and style of eating and living, habitual structures of relating, patterns of gesture and tone of voice—all bear
the marks of mother; and for a woman the mother-complex
comes particularly into play in her self-identity feelings and her
sexual feelings. These influences upon the feeling function do
not have to be copied after the personal mother nor even be
contradictory to her in order for the mother-complex to show
its effect. The mother-complex is not my mother; it is my complex. It is the way in which my psyche has taken up my mother.
Behind is the *Magna Mater.*

Our civilization does not provide adequate vehicles for the
Magna Mater. The positive, nourishing mother does not come
through; we cannot draw sustenance from her in a supermarket,
a modern kitchen, a pornographic book. The cities drain us;
what supports feeling in a day of shopping? What this archetype
could offer as shelter, trust and depth of perspective to the

natural daily round is missing. Where does a woman turn for a model for her feeling function? So, the mother passes on fear and uncertainties to her daughters, since the archetypal mother–daughter mystery and the right kind of awe and am-bivalences have no appropriate place. When Demeter and Persephone are missing, Hecate comes up alone, and there is general fear of the negative feelings: fear of realizing her hatred for her children, the death aspect in her loving, the witchery in her intelligence. How can she trust her feelings when they are so full of "negative" qualities? Where to place her destruction? Without the archetypal perspective, nature receives a one-sided, only-good definition, and everything that does not accord is called "unnatural" and negative.

To study thoroughly the development of feeling under the in-fluence of the mother-complex we would have to move into mythology. That, however, is not the aim of these lectures which are confined to the level of the feeling function within the psychology of consciousness as Jung describes it in his *Psycho-logical Types*. But *Magna Mater* is there nevertheless in those in-tense reactions of many women in regard especially to those feelings having to do with mothering. "I'm not your mother," they enjoy announcing to their man who is down. They deny their children, hate them, refuse to have them, turn to lesbian or manic defenses—anything to prevent becoming "the mother" and experiencing those feelings.

When the intensity of feeling connected to or, better, bound by the mother-complex reaches the proportions of affect, we find the deepest source of feeling. Then the feeling function is not free to operate as an instrument of consciousness, but brings with it violent rages and passionate exaggerations of every sort. These overwhelming affects that swamp the vessel of the feeling function can cause such suffering, such utter help-lessness, that we find ourselves preferring not to feel at all rather than run the risk, each time we attempt to use the feeling function, of the tidal wave on which it is borne. Lest feeling be carried away by reaction, we prefer not to react. So does the mother-complex work toward keeping feeling under the dom-ination of affect and cutting us off from its use.

This situation produces that peculiar laming or crippling of

men with a strong mother-complex. (Dreams show wounded
animals, bleeding, surgical repair on the heart, etc.) All too
familiar is that lack of response, not being able to get started, to
get going, that vague indifference and detachment under which
one intuits a seething tempest. The feeling function then is
often substituted by a feeling mask (persona) of politeness and
mannered consideration which can reach hyperacuity in surface sensitivity and aestheticism. Involvement with a man who is
bound in this way leaves the impression that he is "not really
there." What is not there is a consciousness of his feelings. He is
unable to bring them into the scene. He and the relationship
are always a victim of their whims. Everything is unpredictable,
which is not—though some men may like to believe it—the
same as creatively spontaneous. The question which comes to
the other so naturally at these moments—"How do you feel?"
—if the mother-complex man is able to answer at all, releases a
wave of chaos teeming with every sort of fish: self-pity, sad longings, sexual desire, inflated ambitions, bitter resentments,
kitsch, and then apathy which swallows them all.

Because the expression of feeling is accompanied by a feeling
of loyalty to what has been expressed, the inhibition of expression particularly damages the feeling function. The explosion
of affect has no such accompaniment; we can explode and
forget all about it, no responsibility. But feeling gets us involved
and committed in a curious way to what has been expressed, a
phenomenon which tells much about the way in which the feeling function develops mainly through expressing feeling. The
mother-complex inhibits the expression, as if "she" intended to
prevent any feeling from being used apart from her demands
for affects (or indifference). Feeling must have its source and
goal in "her." (We can judge whether our feeling function is
serving the mother-complex by noting how like or unlike the
forms of our feeling evaluations and reactions are to those of
our actual mother or her substitutes in peer group, class, club,
church, etc.) We can hardly have the feeling function in our own
hands as an instrument of consciousness until we can get it out
of "her" hands as the archetypal dominant of the unconscious,
ruling over the past, the flesh and our inmost intimacy. Hand-to-

hand wrestling with the sword of logos and the manly girdle of action is less successful than the incestuous return.

When therapy speaks of the "incestuous return to the mother," it means going to the emotional depths where the feeling function lies bound. In this union with our emotionality we are at our most intimate and weakest place, but often just here the feeling function has its roots. The incestuous return alone can free feeling to function for me; my feelings here seem to be my own personal belongings, my treasure, as the myths would tell us, that is guarded by the mother-dragon of reptilian coldness and fiery passion, or by the witch herself who can turn us all back into dwarf tree-stumps, little birds a-twitter or just dumb stones. Incest, at this moment in the development of feeling, means allowing oneself to join with the darkest, bloodiest passions, the actual longings to be held and carried and caressed, the uninhibited rages and furies. It is a Tantric way, if we see it through Hindu eyes. One immerses oneself in the *kleshas,* the attachments to the Mother Goddess. It means going where the heart really is, where we actually feel, even if in the fists, guts and genitals, rather than where the heart should be and how we ought to feel.

Many dark things occur in this incestuous return—again the realm of the "mothers" where the feeling function meets with suicidal impulses, despair, dismemberment, a sense of horror and rot (putrefaction), hungry oral needs in the form of desperate cravings and compulsions. Through the return to this level, the feeling function can sort out the values of these experiences and work out a relationship with the psyche's so-called dark side. When this has not been done, when introverted feeling does not function by recognizing the worth of these experiences, then we are victims of the incest. Of signal importance in any crisis or breakdown is the discovery of its *value,* which precedes its meaning. By not valuing our neurotic and psychopathic messes we perpetuate the mess and miss the chance for freeing feeling from the mother.

In the practical situation of a human relationship where one person wants to help another with his feelings, the mother which binds the feelings can be met with the same constellation of mothering. (As Jung says: "For 'what has been spoiled by the father' can only be made good by a father, just as 'what has been spoiled by the mother' can only be repaired by a mother." *Mysterium Coniunctionis, CW* 14, ¶232; cf. *I-Ching,* Hexagram 18.) Constellating the good mother in a relationship means simply to mother, to care for, to take up and nourish and be kind to this weakness, lostness, boyishness or girlishness in the other without oneself feeling threatened and confused, put upon, or becoming hyper-active and therapeutic. Regardless how deep a person may go in chaos and despair, the incestuous return may have a valuable outcome if the partner in the relationship encourages one to go yet deeper. (As with every rule or counsel there are exceptions and definite contra-indications, especially in regard to the mother-complex, since its ultimate depths are archetypally beyond life.) The main point in constellating the good mother is standing below, cradling the fall, so that the fear of disintegration and helplessness is met with support. The support of the positive mother is indiscriminate nourishing. It puts a positive sign on every emotion and every feeling in order to redeem it from exile in guilt and shame. Where a person is reduced to childlike helplessness by the chaos of his emotionality and by the fact that the feeling function, under the stern control of the harsh and critical mother or the subtle poison of the kind Little Old Lady, only admonishes and upbraids, it is the vivid interest on the part of the other which acts like a midwife bringing to birth the new function. The mark of the good mother is not sweet-smelling milk-kindness and the bland diet of acceptance, but *active spirited interest* in whatever is stirring, thereby furthering growth by postponing all discrimination of weed from flower until a later time. She broods all eggs together. It is a subtle trick of the critical mother to choose among nascent feelings, which develops only a susceptibility to premature criticism, crippling the feeling function, nipping in the bud by deciding too soon what is good and bad.

Return to the mother for the sake of feeling cannot help but turn us back into the boy and girl again with that rawness and naiveté of feeling of the boy and girl, quite inadequate yet also authentic. Or, if the return is indicated by explosions or whiny complaints, nourishing here does not mean catering to the neurosis as much as it means connecting with it. By giving value to the anger or the complaint and encouraging its expression by feeling, it moves toward consciousness.

Hero myths show that the development of masculinity seems to be a movement against the mother-complex. But this development takes place not only by means of conquering her through the man's world, overcoming inertia, making decisions and taking a stand. To read and know more, to decide and act more, to build muscle and gain competence in the world of manly men does not make a full man. If the feeling function is not freed, we can be called back home any time. Freedom is shown by access to one's feelings and the use of one's feeling function.

"Manly" men, to show the strength of their feeling, come on brutish, coarse, callous or fakely fatherly. They compensate the lability and sensitivity with thick-skinned nastiness, no weakness showing—until the heart-attack or breakdown. Here, the feeling function has been stylized into a stereotype of a burst of laughter, overt warmth, patronizing pats, or any of the other "manly" ways. But stereotypes are mechanisms; the function is still servant to the mother; it has not come into its own. Thus, the manly man has supporters and attendants who carry his feeling for him, giving him accolades, and power-manipulations affect all his relationships which are based on giving and getting. When the mother-complex governs feelings through this manly compensation, the connection to others has more than a usual amount of bargaining. Within it all is the anxiety of collapse and the need for support.

Since the mother-complex protects one from life, it keeps one from feeling what one feels. Feelings get one involved, so the mother has to keep us from feeling. Life then doesn't quite reach us, and we become untouched and untouchable, partly because we do not feel, partly because we feel so much, every pore a wound. Or, the mother can inflate us, protecting by keeping us up and above, where we lose the human touch.

Such men say, "Don't touch me"; they cannot bear to be held. Being touched, either physically or psychologically, only reminds them of their own inadequate responses, their own inferior feeling. The hardest stand of all for the man struggling with this problem is in favor of his negative feelings, for it is just these which the mother-complex condemns. Just these, therefore, are the ones which give that experience of freedom when admitted and expressed. How free we feel when we can deny a request, explain a dislike, put a long-harbored resentment or irritation into words. The expression of negative feelings through the feeling function brings with it new energy and a sense of liberation. Also, one has been able by feeling what one feels to laugh in the face of the Gorgon and her critical repressive moralisms about feeling.

The paralysis constellated by the mother-complex in all matters where feeling is required is therefore worked at best by discovering one's feelings about people, places, things. The "manly" man lets his wife decide these lesser matters; it is of no concern to him how he feels, and in fact he often doesn't know whether he is happy or sad until some member of the family tells him. The mother within has so long ruled the stereotypes of his feeling in regard to himself and his world that he has no awareness at all of his value as a person, his values, nor of the ethical, aesthetic and relational aspects of his style of life.

Mother-complex interference with the feeling function can be countered by other kinds of manly virtues than the tough ones we have mentioned. For instance: it is important for a person to find feeling values in his actions, not merely giving value to action for its own sake. It is important to feel why and for what purpose, to feel what one wants, whom one likes, and what values are expressed through what one does. It is important to enter situations where there is a conflict of interests to whose solutions the feeling function contributes.

Of most importance is friendship. The ambivalence of the mother-complex is countered by permanency, by loyalty and fidelity. These are virtues of friendship which have always occupied moral philosophers. Aristotle devoted several books to friendship in his *Ethics;* Cicero, Seneca, Plutarch each wrote upon it, and this tradition continues, for example, in Gabriel Marcel's *Creative Fidelity.* No matter how freed a man is, supposedly, of the mother-complex, if he has no friends, merely a superficial multitude of acquaintances, something still interferes with the feeling function. The mother-complex inhibits

loyalties and attachments; it puts questions of trust into the for-
mulas of dependency and betrayal. In order to keep safe and
sure, not to hurt or be hurt, one has many ever-changing friends
and no lasting friendships. Friendship in the classical writers
was said to be reserved for maturity; it represented the ideal
relationship of free and equal men. Because it indicates a redemption of the feeling function from the mother-complex, an
analysis so often wants to turn into a friendship. Analysis,
because it is therapeutic and supportive, constellates the
mother; it is not free as friendship is, so that the urge to become
friends reflects, in part, the need of the feeling function to move
the analytical relationship into a new place. Sometimes it works,
sometimes not.

From the foregoing, we can conclude that emotional chaos is
not to be got rid of or even got through. We may fall into it
again and again as new feeling values appear or as the feeling
function increases its range. The ages of man or stages of life imply continual transitions and new uses of the feeling function.
Because the mother-complex as our fundamental unconsciousness always constellates the ego into its childishness, it is painful
to revert to infantilisms. We fear these falls. One would almost
rather not have feelings at all if they must be gained only in this
way. It is humiliating. Although religions talk much of humility,
they do not tell us what it actually feels like except as a virtue,
which is then no longer humility at all, but a new form of pride.
To be weak and helpless in one's feelings, to stand loyal with
one's negative feelings, to be delivered over to one's childishness—and this in front of another person—is indeed humiliating. There, perhaps, humility begins: in that inadequacy of
inferior feeling; for the humiliation of inferior feeling is the
feeling inferior of humility. In this sense the mother-complex
and its eternal recurrence as fate offer the humility of *amor fati*,
feeling flowing into fate, its limitations and our smallness. With
this idea we come again to the idea that feeling is the art of the
small.

CHAPTER VI
Feeling and the Anima

While we may be clear that the anima-complex is not the feeling function of a man, at the same time we must keep in mind that it, like the mother-complex, has a special relationship with feeling and has responsibility in its disorders. This is a puzzling area for both men and women: men often cannot tell when they are feeling and when they are in the anima; women find themselves drawn by a man's anima-feeling only to find themselves involved in something peculiar. Since the anima by definition refers to the archetypal background of a man's femininity, anima-feeling has characteristics which are strikingly "feminine." They are exaggerations of what we commonly believe to be feminine. If the mother-complex is the chord played by the left hand, setting a fundamental rhythm and key to feeling which the right hand may vary upon but never depart from, the anima-complex is the melody played out of tune, too sharp or too flat, the timing just off.

The femininity of a man is generally personified by images of women or symbols referring to women which act as constellating (fascinating, attracting) dynamisms drawing a man into involvements through which he may discover more about himself and this archetypal reality. These involvements may come as inner moods and fantasies or as projections and projects. However they appear, it is through these compelling interests that a man is led into hitherto unknown, i.e., unconscious, aspects of life. The anima-complex is classically called the mediatrix to the unconscious and is thus a function of *relationship*, like the feeling function.

In its mediatrix function, the anima-complex also performs in a feminine way by receiving and containing the new, relatively unconscious events which are activated. The ability to connect to the unconscious depends altogether upon the capacity to receive and contain what it presents, either inner moods and fantasies or outer projections and projects. The reverse is as well true: the capacity to open and be receptive increases the ability to connect. Inasmuch as a man's feelings are repressed or his feeling function is relatively undeveloped, the anima-complex will compensatorily have that much more feeling-tone and represent that much more of the feeling function. Also, insofar as the anima-complex gives the feeling to a man of his own subjectivity and intimacy, it will be experienced not only in images and projections but also in feelings. This is all the more true in our extraverted and masculine-oriented culture with its collective repression of feeling.

R. B. Onians examines the earliest meanings of the term "anima" (and "animus") in his *The Origins of European Thought* (Cambridge, 1954). He says that there is much confusion about the term "anima." "Animus is concerned with consciousness and anima has nothing to do with consciousness" (p. 169). Anima seems to have been a more generic word applied to anything of the nature of vapor, air, wind, to breezes, exhalations, as well as to the human breath (pneuma, psyche). Above all, anima refers to the *vital principle,* or the principle of life, as Jung has often emphasized. Despite its vapory insubstantiality, the anima comes as a driving force as important as the breath we breathe. Some of its archetypal imagery has been presented by Emma Jung. Other highly elaborated forms of this Goddess of life are represented by feminine figures in Greek myth, especially the Kore figures, and Ariadne, Persephone, Aphro-

Complexes are self perpetuating in their intention (handwritten annotation at top of page)

dite, Artemis. Many other divine and half-divine or legendary women could be mentioned, but the main point in our context is their constellating effect upon the feeling function. The anima involves the feeling function into the turmoil of life, but it is not the same as feeling.

Returning to our distortions of feeling occasioned by the anima-complex, we find that anima-feeling tends to be too *sensitive.* Virginal, reclusive, cautious, it fears being hurt or hurting the other person. For fear of someone's being hurt, feeling matters are shyly veiled and not aired. "Things are better left undiscussed." Much time passes in quiet discretion. Anima-feeling is too *sincere;* feeling becomes heavy, and every feeling-tone given to any experience or idea takes on importance in the grand romantic manner. Then secrets are kept about the wrong things, and issues swell into significance owing to wrong value judgments. (A man, for instance, has an ordinary skiing hut in the Alps, but because of his anima-feelings for it, he invests it with mysterious importance and it becomes a Shangri-La very close to heaven's door.) When a man's own feeling evaluations are lacking, they are easily replaced by anima over-valuations and enthusiasms. Everything is so full of meaning, of religious import, of pompous wisdom. Feeling becomes sincere confessions, sincere goodness of aspiration. Corresponding with a young anima image in a man's dreams, the quality of the sincerity will take on the tones of the college coed.

In this phenomenology also belong the *too polite* feelings. In an exaggeration of harmony and the feminine knack for smoothing things over, polite feeling yields to the other, giving in before tensions mount. It is always adjustedly right. By being always right, it is of course not right, because life is not always right. The conscious feeling function can manage negativity and give discord its due; but anima-feeling wants to avoid trouble since it has not the differentiation to handle feeling complexities. (We must remember: complexes are self-perpetuating in their intention. As energetic nuclei they attract events toward them and tend to bind whatever is not already in some order. Therefore, they tend toward aggrandizement at the expense of differentiation. They tend to lump together and to react all-or-

nothing. The anima, as a complex, thus works against differentiated feeling.)

Anima-feeling is often too *light and charming.* There is always a
laugh and the right remark which cuts the deeper feeling, as if
feeling were a tap dance on twinkle-toes that skirts the edges of
involvement. So, too, anima-feeling shows *vacillation,* not out of
fundamental ambivalence as with the mother-complex but
rather owing to a flirtatiousness with values. Half-values with
half-smiles are proffered. A man wriggles away, flirts with main
issues, lies, and perverts the truth of things for the sake of vanity. Judgments go this way, then that, especially in regard to feelings about life actions, morals, people. The vacillation, the
indecisiveness can be ended only by the logos sword, which the
anima keeps him from using by appealing to his fear of error,
possible loss of prestige, and "hurting someone."

It shows itself too in *auto-eroticism.* Then a man is in love with
his love, feels only his feelings, finds it marvelous that he feels
something at all, which leads to the worship of feeling for its
own sake. Auto-eroticism here refers simply to the anima-
feelings a man has toward himself, his self-love, in which the
anima, as if it were a real woman, continually gushes over him
admiration and fantasies of inflated value about his looks,
achievements and potentialities. Without his own feeling as a
counterjudgment, a man can thus be led to over-extension, disaster and collapse. The same auto-eroticism brought on by the
anima can also lead to an indolent partial paralysis. There will
be fantasies of feeling moves (clearing up a negative situation,
entering a relationship, divorcing, getting married, making a
feeling choice) and preparations rather than actual performance. Or, the performance may be no more than that, a performance staged for oneself, to gain the love of the anima, her
divinely flattering attention.

This auto-eroticism comes out in curious ways. A man invites
a woman over for supper. He has fixed up the room, candles, a
record he likes softly playing, "just the right mood." She comes
in and within ten minutes a fight has started—probably by her.
The anima atmosphere in the room which he believes right-
eously is feeling has oppressed her and blocked her feeling to

such an extent that she comes out with an animus attack to cut the shit. Then they argue about feeling and what it is and who has it and so on. Surely, the man made an effort, but just as surely the anima mood had nothing to do with the feeling function except in terms of his private (auto-erotic) feelings.

Feeling can also become too *aesthetic*, love only for the beautiful, or love only for beautiful women, or the inability to enter into that aspect of feeling where it is harsh and savage. Anima aestheticism cannot shout, yet shouting can belong to appropriate feeling. In Stendhal's *De l'amour* there is a chapter where he speaks of Beauty being dethroned by Love. He refers to that step in the development of the feeling function where the anima-complex, as the worship of Beauty, is replaced by the appropriate feelings of love for a woman. From one point of view, the more important a woman's beauty is to a man, the less individual and personal is the relationship. Over-fondness for usual beauty, from this point of view, is a sign of anima love rather than an expression of the feeling function. Hence the difficulty a beautiful woman has in finding an individual relationship with a man. She is doomed to catching his anima-feeling, and she may be driven to sacrifice her beauty to gain his love. The aesthetic distortion also serves to suppress negative feelings and leaves a man incapable of coping with the tough situations of life where ugliness and plain dirt belong. The aesthetic anima does not like swearing and cursing, suffering dumb animals, the smell of gunpowder, the oppressed poor, the noise of cities and pollution, whereas "her" feelings do go to the beauties of nature, cultured art and religions of incense and song.

Another aspect of anima-feeling is *materialism*. Caught by "her," without a sense of values, we hang on to objects sentimentally. They take on magic through association to the anima-complex. We keep a drawer of mementoes, identifying feelings with material things and giving them mana. Anima-feeling is quickly fascinated by wealth and power, so that the judgments one makes about people have a materialistic aspect, and the people one likes tend to be the "right sort." In this way anima-values tend to favor the persona, the adaptation to collectively approved criteria. The feeling function ascertains values according to the feeling values objectively given to the psyche; but

anima-feeling confuses what is objective with objects, with what is evident, concrete, collective. Therefore, the expression of feeling also becomes materialistic; one has to make a fuss and show, or say it with "things." Giving replaces feeling. We get more occupied with ourselves and our gift than with the other person who finds the gift a claim on his feeling.

The anima-complex has historical associations. Jung often speaks of it in terms of its reaches downward and backward into historical and mythical levels of the psyche. This aspect can also be materialized, so that aesthetic feeling values become distorted into a worship of the past, of antiquity, of classic taste. One expresses one's feeling in collections of pewter or silver, paintings and archeological remnants.

The anima-complex can also distort feeling by making it too *personal*. Where men's interests tend to be impersonal (ideas, plans, facts, things) and where not enough attention is given to the personal and intimate, the anima surreptitiously takes over this part of life. Men fall prey to every sort of petty plotting in personal affairs. They gossip, they politic with values, they watch over their children's personal lives—especially their daughters'—like frightened spinsters with lecherous shadows, ready at any moment to explode with rage or fall into a fit of pique at table. Men cannot get above the personal by simply ignoring it or turning it over to women. Part of the integration of the feeling function is the right connection with the personal, the "just mine." Because standing for this aspect of one's personality (which always has this "just mine," this personal quality) as an affirmation of identity is a risk and an exposure, it is usually more comfortable for a man to let someone else do it for him (a secretary, a wife, a mistress). Unfortunately, the someone else is frequently the anima-complex, and "his" can no longer be separated from "hers." Everything then takes on a monogram and is stamped with a personal idiosyncrasy.

We can partly agree with the classical Jungian position that anima-feeling also shows in *distortions of sexuality:* too much or too little sexuality in the feeling. For some, it seems the feeling function is located in the genitals, and a man only feels where he is attracted, so that when desire departs feeling does too. Closer analysis of this condition shows, however, an alliance be-

antinomian – one who rejects a socially established morality
antinomy = paradox
priapic (L. leecher): phallic

tween the shadow side of masculinity and the anima. (Anima sexuality is usually not this "low," this "instinctual," but has all sorts of sentimental, hyperaesthetic, mental ideas about sex, sex on the mind, or full of "heart," rather than a direct expression of the genitals.)

Sexualized feeling is represented in the dreams by shadow figures and by the anima-complex who favors them. She goes off with the dark man in the dream, or constellates rape, or calls up longings that combine holy heights with sexual titillation. The anima seems particularly to like the antinomian and pseudo-guru mixtures of sexuality and spirituality, where the priapic shadow is disguised under the robes of the holy-man and where feeling makes a metaphysical virtue of socially disruptive behavior. People no longer then merely love and are jealous, enter triangles and have affairs, as people have always done; instead they justify what goes on with a "new morality," "tantric experiences," "free love," "individuation," and other doctrines derived by the feeling function and supported by the anima.

The pseudo-feeling of these doctrines can easily be detected because negative feelings have been suppressed. Jealousy is "overcome," power and petty fussing and the narrowing that occurs within intense relationships are all coated over with higher ideals. While encouraging the shadow of desire, the anima leads a man into a less obvious shadow. People used to call this "turning one's head"; the anima turns a man's attention—for better and for worse—through the manipulation of feeling so that he may be in the "worse" yet sees only the "better." The honesty of his desire is replaced by the dishonesty of his philosophical justifications about it. Here, jealousy can be the saving grace, for jealousy has the one great virtue of producing a kind of psychological honesty. It keeps a triangle authentically difficult, down to basic passions of the psyche, hatred, murder and fear. The shadow is right there, without Sugar's sugar-coating. Aphrodite never came without troubles in the tales; she had dark sisters, the Furies, and she was served by Custom, Grief and Anxiety.

We agree only partly with the classical position that the anima sexualizes feeling, because sometimes the Jungian position neglects the importance of sexuality in feeling. If feeling is archetypally connected with Eros, it will have echoes at the psy-

Jealousy is coated with new ideals!

choid level. For feeling to reach the complexes and represent them, it must also have a body component, even if not molar and massive in the sense of affect and emotion. I do not mean to confuse body with sexuality, for body consciousness is not always sexual and sexuality can be very mental, yet we ought not go too far in making separations between feeling and sexuality. Too easily one falls for the notion that "good feeling" is purged of sexuality and desire.

Quite possibly sexuality has its own feeling aspect which is more than the feelings that are awakened through sexuality. This feeling function works as an inhibitor or guide within any instinctual force, providing it with its own laws. These laws may differ from the moral laws imposed upon sexuality—how it "should" perform and what feelings one "should" have. Feeling may direct and elaborate sexuality as in the mating games of animals or in our complicated courting patterns, love-letters and divorce procedures. At what moment two people go to bed, or cease going to bed, is determined by feeling as much as by sexuality, and here feeling acts as a *spiritus rector* of the instinct, just as the instinct acts through feeling.

I have tried to discuss the natural and inherent self-inhibition of compulsion in two papers: "Towards the Archetypal Model for the Masturbation Inhibition" and "On Psychological Creativity." This offers another way of regarding feeling: it can be conceived as a reflective component of instinct, just as each God has his ritual requirements and feeling "laws" for observing his cult. These thoughts move the theme of these chapters beyond the notion of feeling as a function of consciousness. Here, we are suggesting a meta-psychological emphasis, feeling as an archetypal phenomenon per se, akin to conscience and self-regulation. As Jung wrote (*CW* 8, ¶ 411), the archetype has a feeling aspect or always has an effect upon feeling. We can make this precise by suggesting that each archetype delivers to consciousness a load of feelings of different kinds and also works upon the feeling function in general by both compelling it and inhibiting it with awe of the numinous, a holy fear, a reflective moment of carefulness.

Certain consequences follow from this: if feeling might be a component of instinct as represented in the reflective ritualization of instinct, then ritualization of sexuality would be a way of reinforcing the feeling aspect. The sexual anima who so likes the shadow man, demanding ever more sexuality in the feeling, can go through a process of sexual ritualization in order to release the feeling reflection and inhibition. Many of the most perverse forms of sexuality, including the descriptions of de Sade, can be seen as attempts to draw out the feeling level of sexuality, to make sexuality a reflection of the psyche rather than only an activity of instinct.

I do believe that common language gives a psychoid level to feeling; that is, it emphasizes the relation between the feeling function and body-consciousness. When people describe where they feel, they put a hand on the chest or gut, clench a fist, or droop their shoulders in depression. Feeling can be abstract, ethical, aesthetic, diplomatic, political—all the areas we have mentioned. It can be as cold and clear and precise as thought; nevertheless, there is this peculiar body component to feeling, so that any feeling reaction that is not in tune with the body serves to sever us from the body. Unfortunately, a great deal of what passes for feeling is "made up" niceness, without body-consciousness in it, and acts schizogenically upon its recipients and its donors.

The same sort of psychology holds true for the animus. It can manipulate feeling and ally itself with the woman's shadow desires for power-through-sex. How often women are abused by those men who come at them with gentle, fatherly, tender, considerate feelings, taking the elbow as they cross the street, lighting their cigarettes first, the intimate word in the ear. These men are supposed to be lovers; they make a woman "feel good." When feeling is functioning, this sort of thing is laughed off the stage. But too often it flatters an inferior function to be given these gross demonstrations of "good feeling," by means of which the animus and shadow are manipulating toward a scene that may well end in crushing betrayal or a furious fight over money.

As we too often insist the anima has to do with eros and feeling, so we mistakenly identify the animus with logos and ideas. But the animus, especially in therapy where so much is made of feeling, can well manifest as a feeler, and again, like anima-feeling, it will be just off. All the values and all the heart will be peculiarly half-values and half-hearted. This pseudo-feeling of the animus creeps into many analytical sessions as soon as the people try to "express their feelings." Key words for detecting the animus are "really," "my own," "good," "positive," "related" —and the word "feeling" itself.

Lastly—and not because we have come to an end but only to decide for a stop—anima-feeling, lacking the individuality of ego expression, is frequently *undirected*. Then a man suffers from *Weltschmerz*, vague cosmic feelings, poetry in insubstantial images, a fondness for flowers and stars, clichés that could have been written by anyone, anywhere to anyone, anywhere. Feeling leaves the immediate reality altogether and no longer connects with the moment and the matter at hand. Undirected feeling, although it feels for groups and problems of groups and the larger ideas which disturb the world, wanders from the point at issue. It is *irrelevant*—perhaps because it has no body in it, and so nobody is there.

An example of this irrelevance. A man and a woman go out for dinner. He is correct and polite with her yet excessively entertaining with the waitress whom he has never seen before nor will ever see again. Underneath he is angry with his companion, but it appears only indirectly through the charm he puts on for the waitress. The woman then expresses the anger for him as a result of the anima manipulation which lets him off scot-free, still a polite gentleman. This example also shows how the anima can make use of feelings that are not expressed, distorting them into devious channels for troublesome ends.

All these distortions from which a man suffers, and from which the women in his life are forced to suffer even more, are used for feeling and pass for feeling, but cannot be attributed to the feeling function. By definition it is a function of consciousness: it is more or less available to consciousness depending upon the type orientation of the personality. But theoretically it is available as a conscious instrument to each, regardless of type. *Its weakness and delay in appearing can be charged against the mother-complex, while substitutions for it are the result of the anima-complex.* The former distortions we bring with us from childhood and are part of its curse and our pain. But we have no personal blame. The latter distortions, however, are more serious because they reveal not what we could not do in our helplessness, but that which we would not do in our cowardice. Where the conscious personality does not have the courage to risk with feeling, the anima intervenes with its falsifications. These falsifications as sketched above have one essence in common: they are selfish, self-reflecting, self-satisfying. This is little wonder, since it is the function of the anima to give the experience to a man of being connected to his center, related to himself; or, as it is phrased in classical Jungian language, the anima relates the ego to the Self. In anima-feeling, this is done in a devious way, leading neither to consciousness nor to relatedness, but rather to an inflated sense of self. Where the anima does help the feeling function, however, is precisely through these difficulties, for the anima brings conflict, disorder and falsification, providing the feeling function a place to exercise its main activity: the discrimination of values and the elaboration of relationship.

The aid another can give to releasing feeling from anima distortion is to step in naturally, replacing the complex. This means the other must recognize and give importance to that experience of my most central value. For the anima always feels like "me" in a man. She points to my mystery. Hence through that complex we are so touchy, so ready to be led into inflations, ambitions, and the satisfaction of strong desires. If no one else can truly see me with the vision I need in order to find myself, or connect with interest to a Self too mysterious for me to recognize, then I fall for the anima's feelings and am led astray—which too, as Oscar Wilde observed, has its advantages ("The advantage of the emotions is that they lead us astray").

CHAPTER VII

Education of the Feeling Function

Schooling tends mainly to develop the functions of thinking and sensation, although intelligence tests with their emphasis on quickness and guessing favor intuition. Feeling education, in the sense of taste, values, relationships, is not the core of schooling. Music, art, sports, social clubs, religion, politics, drama, reading for pleasure—these are elective and extracurricular. Where can the heart go to school? Perhaps it was not so preposterous to claim that the profession of psychotherapy owes its existence to the inadequate and undeveloped state of the feeling function in general.

The development of the feeling function through psychotherapy would not be so necessary had our usual education included feeling more in its aims. Rousseau said: "He among us who can best carry the joys and sorrows of life in my opinion is the best educated." The education of the rational mind, much as we have been led to believe by the indoctrination of schooling, little makes us capable of coping with joys and sorrows. Rather the contrary is true: the education of the rational mind makes us less able with feeling, since feeling and thinking would seem, for the most part, to develop at the expense of each other. The Romantics knew this and said: "Feeling may err but it can only be corrected by feeling" (Herder). This statement denies the superiority of the reason of the mind over the reason of the heart and presents the Romantic threat to Classical order. Inferior feeling cannot be corrected from above by superior thinking. The beginning of feeling education is turning a deaf ear to one's superior functions, whose disapproval—even if tolerantly educative—of whatever is less acts mainly repressively. Feeling requires an *education through faith*; it begins to function only when we can trust it to function and allow it its errors.

The psyche works at its own errors by means of its self-steering, self-correcting tendency. It leads us, in dreams especially, back to adolescence where the problems of feeling become acute and where the educational system in which we have passed all those long days fails these problems totally. Until adolescence, feeling development is given more attention in that the child is both allowed more and directed more. But at adolescence, without initiations and taboos, without instruction or forms, we are turned loose into the secular turmoil of the world, bringing to it our own contribution of chaotic feelings.

Accordingly, the return to adolescence in the dreams of adults often points to gaps of forgotten feelings, where the affective life was beginning to open and the feeling function beginning to make differentiations, only to have its values twisted by ignorance and repressed by fear. Dreams take one back again to where it went wrong, back to school—but this time for the education of feelings.

So we find the homosexual and lesbian connections and fantasies, the repetitive appearances of certain teachers, the high school loves, and the recollections of people so trivial and remote in memory but who insist on returning through dreams mainly for the feeling characteristics that they embody. Rather than growing out of the adolescence—as we might like to believe is the intention of the analytical process—we find ourselves growing backward through an adolescence relived again: songs, scenes, faces that touch the heart with an extraordinarily vital, even if sentimental, pull.

A first step in the education of feeling is lifting the repression of fear. The feelings must first be caught and held in consciousness and recognized as feelings. Since it is the feeling function which feels feelings, it must be allowed to feel what it actually does feel as it happens, admitting and accepting, without the intervention of superior functions. Not only the superior functions interfere. Feeling itself judges the psyche's contents with narrow evaluations. Our own stale moralisms, cheap tastes and intolerances work against us. It is as if feeling develops through suspension of itself, holding in abeyance so that we can newly reflect rather than habitually judge what we feel.

The education begins when I begin to trust my own spontaneous first feeling—"I don't like his face," "I feel mixed up," "I don't feel anything," "I just feel angry but at nothing in particular"—regardless of whether or not this first feeling is generally admissible and acceptable in the collective system of values. When I repress the simplest feeling reactions, I prevent the feeling function from developing these contents into discriminated evaluations. For example, if I repress for moral reasons ("I am married and I ought not feel such desires," "It's wrong of me to hate him for no reason at all"), nothing further can come of my feelings; they remain nipped and stunted. Or, for example, depressive feelings get me and I say: "we all feel like this sometimes," which is another one of those habitual clichés that prevents the specific movement of that specific depression from showing what it wants.

These little mechanical defenses against feeling keep it attached to its affective roots, for anything newly coming into consciousness comes with a potential that is more affectively charged than the ego-system itself, else it would not make itself felt, could not get in. Before the animal can be tamed, it must be caught. Before education can proceed, there must be something to educate. This implies a responsibility toward one's feeling, whatever it feels like, and not only a responsibility to the ideals of how one should feel. This responsibility in fact puts to the test one's ideals, for it requires courage and honesty to give place to all that a feeling would say once it is let in.

It is not what contents a person carries in his unconscious that reveal his character, for we have our statistical share of the bomber, murderer and pervert, but how one meets these contents. The criminal-twist that each complex has as part of its potential is a shock to feeling. I may ignore this shock and simply not feel that shadow of my nature. Or I may play social-worker toward my criminality, trying to help and understand; or the ego may play high-court judge or policeman. As the bomber is within, so is the "pig" who violently represses every sign of violence, never allowing an explosion, clubbing into insensate stupidity with pills, drink and distractions every exaggerated confrontation that the complexes would constellate. How one connects to the anti-social and criminal contents demonstrates one's facility with the feeling function.

Feeling thus requires *psychological courage.* There is civil, moral, physical and intellectual courage—so too a courage of the soul to encounter itself. To meet the contents one carries, to recognize the destruction in one's complexes, and to undergo— which means as well to go under—the disintegration and absent places of one's inferiority call for courage of no small degree.

Psychological courage is a courage of the heart, for we may regard courage as a phenomenon of eros which stands in defense of the heart, both its generosity and its folly. The courage of feeling toward the phenomena of the soul, regardless of what they are, is an enactment of the Eros and Psyche tale, because eros gives love and encouragement to all the contents of the soul which it feels inferior about. The more we stand for eros, the more psychological strength we seem to gain, demonstrating that eros is indeed a dynamus, not only in its desirous portion but altogether as a life-embracing impetus. Courage shows in the feeling function's willingness to take on whatever comes up.

This education through faith and courage can be sabotaged by analytical cleverness. Then we analyze what we feel, too soon trying to figure it out: why, where it came from, what it "means." Then, instead of feeling, we call what we feel a projection and try to "take it back," or take it to the other person to "discuss." Everything, anything but the courage to live the feeling function's inferiority.

Because feeling has both plus and minus sides, acceptance means as well those with the negative sign: deception, dislike, coldness, hatred, sorrow. Negative feelings and their expressions belong equally to the function. As Rousseau said, "the joys and *sorrows* of life"—not the joys alone. The marriage vows, which clearly state feeling values, acknowledge the place of negative feeling: "for better and for worse."

Marriage provides a vessel for negative feelings of every sort, even about marriage itself. Although we may delusionally go into a marriage propelled by thrusts of hope, desire and joy, the elaboration of marriage means bad temper, sarcasm, wheedling, meanness, boredom, and so many complexities of negative feelings that marriage offers a superb vehicle for the feeling function. There are few places where we have the opportunity for a forced, prolonged relationship: jobs we quit, neighborhoods we move from, loves often fade when the wind blows cold. But marriage seems ideally made for the expression of every sort of negative feeling and thus for the differentiation of the feeling function. The fact that marriage seems the only place that these feelings are permitted, even expected, raises the question whether marriage might not be today forced to carry more than its share of both negative feelings (which have no other sanctified place) and inferior functioning (which may not be shown outside). It is a standard joke of feeling that a man keeps up the front all day long only to come home to disintegrate in self-pity and vicious attacks on the family. Of course marriage cannot be a "success" in the old-fashioned sense of a beautiful, loving, growing thing like a tree, just because of these negative feelings which thrive in the relationship of the couple. Yet, marriage is a success when it can live from these negativities and offer to the feeling function a chance for daily exercise. Marriage offers a chance for developing the feeling function because as an archetypal vessel it stands impersonally outside and implacably above whatever takes place within the relationship. The vessel may feel like a trap or cage in which the woman "can't breathe" and the man wants "out," but these experiences testify to the solidity of the impersonal structure. The vows of faithfulness and dedication do not mean the exclusion of the inferior person with his renegade, destructive feelings; the vows mean rather that the inferior person be "married" too, that is, brought into the home and the bed, met with credit rather than suspicion, given an opportunity within marriage to feel just what he or she feels (cf. A. Guggenbühl-Craig, *Marriage: Dead or Alive*, Spring Publ., 1977).

The education of the feeling function for the feeling type may even be more difficult than those with another superior function. After all, the superior function does not age well; it is the adaptedly smooth system that copes, whereas personality development usually takes new steps through its breakdowns of habit where the inferior parts have a chance to come forward. Feeling may extend its range to ever new areas of life, new people, new interests and activities, but unless there is a further differentiation of *values*, where they advance in subtlety and human comprehension, the function itself does not move, only the focus of its attention. Therefore, the feeling type often must suspend his superior function and its values in order to extend the function. A woman feels her son's mistake in marrying a negress; a wife sees the destructive aspect of her husband's best friend; a husband finds waste in his wife's social life. Each of these judgments has much going for it. Yet, by including the position of the son the mother has a chance to discover new values. By judging the husband's friend the wife misses her opportunity to be led by her husband's "inferior" feeling for his "inferior" friend into an area of life that also has values.

The function may have to develop "against its better judgment." Here, perversity can be a way: Swift, Baudelaire, Proust show the potential for the development of feeling through peculiarities and sophistications of what convention says is "good feeling." In a predominantly Protestant culture where sincerity, simplicity and naiveté are given high place, the sophistication of feeling through perversity, aestheticism, irony, exuberance, cunning, and other such ways seems to be "bad" feeling. But we must continually recall that we have a rather impoverished and sentimental notion of an educated feeling function.

In this respect, feeling may require education through the reverse of the usual values—through *lying*, for instance. Truth is not an abstract principle only; it is also the reality of a concrete situation in which various values are operative. What may be the truth in a factual thinking sense may be a lie in order to protect higher values or to be true to the concrete situation. Parents conceal from their children and lie to them, yet expect their children always to tell the truth. Let us say there is a feeling truth and a thinking truth, and sometimes they clash. Then we have the classical conflicts between Mercy and Justice or be-tween Love and Truth. Psychological truth is usually duplex if not complex; that is, it has many sides and therefore many truths. Hermes, who is the leader of souls, the one who points the way for psychological development, begins his life as a newborn child by stealing and lying. Sometimes the individual finds his initiation into psychic reality and its manifold truth to be via a peculiar situation where he is obliged to lie and where his feeling function suddenly is faced with conflicts between the principles of conscience and the necessities of psychological truth.

This problem can be difficult for the feeling function if it has not developed a sophistication and found a connection be-tween the values of the soul and the values of society. The feel-ing type usually reflects the established values of a civilization, incorporating them into principles of conscience. He feels him-self part of the law and supports the doctrine of truth that has resulted from a historical process. The relation to the values of society is another manner in which feeling can develop. Com-fortable acceptance or absolute rejection shows the all-or-none reaction of inferiority.

Where only a few years ago a good deal of psychotherapy had as its goal the extraverted feeling aims of adjustment to the values of external reality, now it has turned to the introverted goals of adjustment to internal values. There has been a sharp conversion from extraverted to introverted feeling. Before we adjusted the inner man with his symptoms and emotional de-mands for the sake of harmony with job, marriage, school, and society. Now, we dismiss the claims of squaring with society for the sake of adjusting to subjective images, affects and ideas.

But adjustment of one's subjectivity may prove as difficult as getting on with society. My affects and ideas can give me as much trouble as do other people. So, development of the feel-ing function refers as well to this relationship with the "inner," or psychic, world through feeling-fantasies. The "others" with whom one has to get along are also the little people of the com-plexes, and how much does feeling give to their needs? The introverted feeler does place value here; he puts time in on him-self, developing his reactions and judgments and connecting with his relationship fantasies. He connects to his *fantasies* of other people before other people. This takes time, and feelers are often silent; but in the time and silence they develop secur-ity and power.

On the other hand, the non-feeling types undermine them-selves by neglecting the value of what takes place in their psy-chic world—dreams, symptoms, fantasies, depressions—or by tending to put there only negative values. They use their intro-verted feeling to sabotage themselves. They feel guilty about their dreams or regard as trivial and wasteful the moods and fantasies that come spontaneously. They put down moods alto-gether, ignoring that moods, as emotions, carry body with them. They do not give high value to their own soul-stuff. But these feeling-fantasies image my nature, and when I give value to them, they give me value, security and strength. Without this ad-justed introverted feeling, I tend to dislike myself—or will be sustained by an indiscriminate self-love called inflation.

Very often dreams show figures that evoke feeling. These poor, unwanted, ill, and outcast fantasy personalities reflect a condition of the personality and the kind of attention required from the feeling function. In a first conversation with an anima-figure, a man, who had already been in analysis nearly three years, found that the figure demanded only from him that he recognize her with feeling, e.g., that he appreciate her, do things for her, take her into account (be connected with her) in all his activities. A woman analysand was ever and again battling with a "man in dark-glasses" who saw everything darkly. This dream image was the personification of her anxieties and depressions. She viewed him and these moods through his own dark-glasses, seeing the negative states only negatively. But one day she asked him in fantasy what was wrong with his eyes, why he was blind, why he suffered and what she could do for him (rather than ex-pecting the figure to serve her will). A change began to take place. The crippled animus, weak anima, sick hero, hurt child ask not only for amplification through intuition, or interpreta-tion by thinking, but especially for appreciation by feeling.

In the analytical emphasis upon negativity and inferiority, the general notion is that one brings to the hour the darkest perversions, incest-longings, violences and anxieties, and so we tend to lose the importance of heights. Sometimes, in close relationships, as between married partners or fathers and sons, what touches most deeply and inspires most highly is left out. Not only is the dark kept out of the family circle but also the light. The refinement of the function cannot take place without testing the function in regard to the exquisite, the tender, the ecstatic, the grieving. The sparks that really move me as feeling-convictions, which keep me alive and on which my life as a man hangs—do they not belong within a relationship? Are they not also to be expressed as well as my rage and morbid depressions? Does tenderness only belong when the shades are drawn, fury when drunk, tears in a man only at a graveside? Often in an analysis the deeper or higher feelings of love, or belief in oneself, or longing for salvation or the ability truly to love others are the prime movers. We are as much victims of inferior feeling in regard to exuberance as to aggression. We cannot take too much excitement without feeling guilt and anxiety.

In other times, the grand, positive feelings of joy also were ritualized: a time for celebration, for carnival; collective forms for feeling were provided in terms of a divinity. How hard we have it to give exorbitant praise, to pull the magnanimous gesture, or to bask in what wholly makes us happy. We do not let ourselves sing, not merely because of a puritan morality or a super-ego, but because the function cannot sing, and in the bourgeois, secular language of factional psychology, to let go is a sign of immaturity and inflation. The Gods must keep their distance and not enter the living room.

The *creation of atmosphere* also belongs to our topic. The feeling function gives value to a situation. It appraises, judges, and recognizes what values are inherent in the situation and can lead us then to function according to these values. Often the atmosphere is ruined by overvaluing with great expectations or undervaluing with recollective associations that only distract from what is immediately present. Then we feel that whatever is going on in this room with these people is not "it"; "it" is with someone else, at another time, in another place. These *feeling fantasies* sabotage the moment by not giving due value to it. The recognition of value in a situation creates the atmosphere of importance without secondary efforts of decoration, dinner, or dress. Attentive listening alone gives intensity. Feeling in this context is an awareness of "now" and "here." "It" is right where you are. At its height this is the atmosphere of the mystery and the mood of the Mass. Atmosphere is created by the evaluative focus brought to the moment. At another extreme are the family evenings of boredom and the parties torn by "interesting discussion." But these too are feeling atmospheres, and what mainly matters is the mirroring, the recognition of what is happening as it happens. The feeling-types know how to mirror. They can bring out the best in a situation simply by the way they place their attention. They can suffocate the inappropriate and manipulate a conversation by the same method of placing values and showing or withholding interest.

Mirroring is not only reflecting with the mind; it is as well something that happens in the body. It is a presence in posture, a registration in the flesh of events as they take place, those stomach swishes of fear or excitement, the blood draining from hands and feet in coldness, the exhaustion from prolonged tension. In itself this is the sensation aspect of mirroring, yet feeling draws values from these reports and makes its judgments.

The education of feeling involves also the observance of *objective patterns of relationship*. There are rules, for instance, about the relationship of guest and host, of senior and junior, between master and servant, between friends, even between husband and wife. In many cultures these forms of feeling are worked out in great detail. They describe archetypal feeling positions that can be transposed into other situations, even metaphorical and mystical, such as the feeling of bride for bridegroom or the feeling of being a "guest" or a "servant."

We find it difficult to observe objective patterns, especially when they are hierarchical. To hold a superior position without either arrogance or obsequiousness, to give an order without its turning into either a request for a favor or a command, to observe filial piety without succumbing to the family complex

—these are beyond our usual capacities and are not educational aims in a society of democratic individualism.

These patterns would seem to have little to do with feeling, especially the feelings of love which, if its commandment be followed—whether that of Jesus or Aphrodite—like death is the great leveler; all forms of the objective order are obliterated. Love as an emotion is contrary to all structures and functions of consciousness, even feeling. This affect or emotion of love may infuse and transform the feeling function, but it cannot replace it. Love is archetypal, belonging to the Gods and given by them as Eros. *Agape* and *caritas*, too, are associated with religion; that is, they too are a grace originating beyond the human. But feeling does not depend upon the Gods; it is not a force, but an awareness, not a redemption, but an instrument. And odd as it may sound to love's devotees, we can feel and have educated feeling without love, but we cannot love and have educated love without feeling. The affect of love is a simplification; feeling is a differentiation. Where love joins by fusion, feeling connects through discrimination. The patterns of these differentiations are coded in feeling forms that endure beyond the emotional movements of love. Community, the brotherhood of all men, or utopian societies of friends based on love all fall down because of the mistaken notion that love conquers all and can replace the forms of feeling.

The oppositions between Classical and Romantic express less a difference between head and heart than a difference between feeling and love, between the endless order of subtle feeling differentiations and the endless waves of love's emotion that wash all walls away between this and that, right and wrong, ugly and beautiful, you and me. By falling-in-love we can reverse all values and climb up to pinnacles beyond good and evil. Feeling, as a function of consciousness, has a discriminatory Logos aspect which it is the purpose of the Great Goddess to overcome. She would end discrimination and separation. Therefore, the education of the feeling function does not by necessity have to go via falling-in-love, as the dream of romance and the Romantic dream of inferior feeling pretend.

Yet experience tells—the analytical transference is one example—that falling-in-love can and does produce a major development of the feeling function, and we must explore this a bit further. Falling-in-love has an indirect, not a direct, effect upon the feeling function. The direct effect, mistaken for true feeling development, is the sudden experience of so many positive feelings. But their expression, under the intense domination of the love emotion, may still be over-subjective and distorted by love's inflation. And even when these positive feelings are felt and expressed adequately, this is more the gift of love itself and is an archetypally ritualistic part of anyone's behavior, impersonally, unconsciously, when he enters the state of being-in-love. The real development is later and indirect, when feeling begins its long appraisals and discriminations of what is going on, sorting out the feelings and responding to and from them. Then a refinement of the function takes place. Hence we find the value for psychology of love-letters and love-poems and love-diaries. Hence the food a love-affair gives for hours of digestive reverie. Hence, too, the broadened tolerance and understanding for others which a love-affair yields as a late product.

The main educative effect falling-in-love has on the feeling function is that through this experience we come to trust our feelings. This is the education by faith mentioned earlier. In love, we risk our feeling and trust its functioning. Falling-in-love not only opens the door to that host of tender, comical, savage, exalted feelings; it also affords a safe place where these, and others more infantile and more suspect, can be allowed in trust. In love we give value also to the weak, possessive, vain, and clinging feelings. No matter what they feel like, we believe in them and give credit to them since they are the stuff of the affair. Having been received in a situation where they are accepted, we are able to accept them ourselves. The credit the other person gives to us teaches us to believe in ourselves as feeling beings. With this comes the sense of redemption: that our feelings, our heart are "good" and that even the feeling wounds of childhood and adolescence can be risked to exposure, experienced, and healed. To be in love makes us young again partly because it does return us to these wounds of negative feelings and their blurted, bleeding expression, redeeming them by finding for them acceptance within the structure of a relationship.

Falling-in-love yields so many feelings that the feeling function is constellated; else we cannot find our way through. It is put to the test each time lovers meet. No other function can substitute: we cannot think or puzzle out love's maze with perceptions. Because falling-in-love tends to wipe out feeling distinctions, the feeling function is required to organize love. The experience of falling-in-love, where one is thrown into one's feelings and onto one's feeling function, is the overwhelmingly convincing proof that the feeling function exists as an independent, irreplaceable psychological agent.

Personal relationships require personal feeling. Here, the emphasis is on the small. The mystics can instruct us. We like to believe that the great mystics occupy themselves with the vaster cosmic things, but they usually talk about small things, very small things. With the feeling function they reduce intellectual speculation to matters close at hand, personal issues of food and nature. Their laughter is born from trivia. Our spoiled feelings are usually resentments over small things, those little mistakes that have been neglected as one goes along. Then life turns sour: one has soured one's life by missing the small feeling opportunities and one is left with festering minor irritations. To miss the small is to miss with one's feeling function. Therefore, personal feeling needs to be expressed in small ways: personal favors, personal sharing, personal remarks about exactly what one likes in the other. The feeling function, by recognizing the other person's virtues, connects him to these parts, giving him belief in himself. Personal feeling is also expressed in small ways with *eyes, voice,* and *hands.* The shift from one function to another is often given just in the change in tone of voice. As the animus commands and the anima complains, so the feeling function usually has slowness. (It can of course be "put on" in the fake style.) The feeling function can pass through the eyes; some theories of friendship use the image of "face to face" for their model. And hands go beyond words whether in gesture, in aggression, or in soothing the sick.

The use of first names once also expressed personal feeling, but like much else this form has fallen. In "primitive" society the use of names is usually highly ritualized. One often has many names, and the titles of family members are tied with the forms of relationship appropriate to each. In the German-speaking world, appellations differentiate degrees of personal intimacy. One has a title and a first name and perhaps a nickname too. In addition, there are the two forms of "you," all of which offers many combinations. A tale tells that only God knows our true names, yet in today's society we take other people's names into our mouths at first encounter. The name in the mouth of another person is an archetypal expression of feeling. (It signifies intimacy; so for instance a dream once told a man, after he had fallen in love and kissed the woman for the first time, that his name had been engraved on her tongue.) In Proust there is a passage where the first time his beloved mentioned his name he felt as if he had been held naked in her mouth.

The objective patterns of relationship are codified in *manners*. Learning manners means learning forms of feeling. Again, it can be argued that what one really feels has little to do with manners. Manners, it would seem, prevent feeling, because feeling has come to mean a breakthrough of sincerity, putting aside all manners, and "coming out with it," "feeling it like it is." Problems of human contact between black and white, between revolutionary and establishment have reached the place of non-negotiable demands where manners are a laugh! To make a case for manners in a historical period of violence points up the difference between feeling and affect. (Not that feeling cannot also be a conduit for aggression, as in cruelty, brain-washing, or the code of the military.)

Yet manners at their best oppose only affect, not feeling. Feelings which seem too deeply personal for manners reveal the inadequacy of our manners, that they have lost touch with their original purpose. For manners, whether polished or pioneer, give to feeling a form in which it can be understood and received. They offer feeling channels for communication; even the negative feelings of insult and spleen can be passed on by manners. Through the adroit use of them we can freeze, snub, hurt, and ridicule, or show off to arouse envy. That manners become dry, that they reflect only persona, that they become mannered and lose all content and connection with sensitivity only confirm the primary thesis of this chapter: the feeling function is in decay. A standard sign of psychological decay is the split into polarities. On the one hand we have blunt and pregnant feelings, on the other, manners emptied of all service but defense.

The rediscovery of the archetypal significance of manners as necessary and viable channels rather than protective moats would re-ritualize them and give to the careless acts of every day an aspect of ceremony. We would feel with certainty about the simplest aspects of daily life—how to behave and what is expected. Manners would give us the "manner" of dealing. Instead, we must give worried time to molding for each inconsequential thing its own form, or we abandon all such feeling efforts, leaving it to the mothering mass of democratic fellow-feeling which is always supposed to "understand what I meant by that." ("The general mess of imprecision of feeling / Undisciplined squads of emotion"—does Eliot not refer to decayed manners?) The obsessive worry with which we confront daily decisions of feeling, to the profit of advertisers and advisers who batten on our uncertainty, is the result of feeling forms having fallen into unconsciousness. Unlived ritual becomes unconscious obsessions and compulsions.

Manners are archetypally connected with the numinous; they imply a relation to power. They appear at their most elaborate where power is concentrated: in the church, the military, the government, or in the contest of powers, e.g., law courts, sports, aboard ship, in surgery. Manners are usually associated with the mistaken idea of ceremony as something bloodless, courtly and staged. But the "staginess" of manners manifests the numinosity within all life, the archetypal powers which like Gods are within every situation, giving it drama. So, through revitalizing manners we could return to an archetypal sense of social situations, both less personal and more numinous, where what we say and do is carried beyond the power of our individual limits by the import of the manner in which each act is done.

Manners are part of *adjustment*. As we can read in Jung, extraverted feeling is primarily concerned with concord, consideration, compromise. External values are recognized and adjusted to. Adjustment implies such feeling values as joining in and taking part, sharing and helping, and the affirmation of external social reality. Moreover, it means letting go of personal reservations, standing out and standing off. Yielding to the impersonal collective unconscious need not take place only through powerful personal experiences of love, arts, crowds, and religion. It can also be accomplished by submitting to the collective, for the outer collective is an archetype in itself as well as being an arena for all the archetypal forces that are as well within the psyche. Adjustment to the outer collective reduces us to the small proportions of statistical significance. We are indeed then only one of millions, only all too dependently human and creaturely. Threatening as this may be to romantic notions of individuality and our personal hero myth, it is an experience that challenges the feeling function to adjust without justifications, to submit without going under.

Adjustment in the last analysis means appropriate behavior, the "fittingness" of which Plato speaks, the "conduct" of the *I-Ching*. That such a simple thing should be an ultimate art of life shows to what depths the problem of the feeling function can lead us. "Appropriate," a word we have been fond of using in describing developed or superior feeling, refers to one's own individual style and tact in behavior.

Style and *timing* too belong to objective forms of feeling. Stylized is of course the same as mannered; we will encounter it in the decayed extravagances of extraverted feeling as it dries, tending toward the repetitive, insistent, and ornate. As ornamentation begins with simple symbolic inscriptions touched with strong affect and later develops into arabesques and rococo curlicues, so is stylized feeling a late phase in the organization of passion. Nevertheless, it remains within the realm of feeling. (Too easily we reject mannerisms as brittle, cheap, or sentimental, forgetting that these too present feelings and qualities.)

But style is more than stylization. Style is that happy union of individual feeling adjusted to external expectations. It is the feeling function itself, expressing personality as the glass shows off the wine. Or, it is the personality coming through the feeling function so that what is in keeping with one's style is appropriate both for the inner truth of feeling and the outer world. Style is not to be bought in vogues, nor can it even be taught, although it is the thing that those in search of feeling education want so badly. It is the style of a writer the young poet apes sedulously, the style of the lecturer the student imitates, the style of the analyst the patient carries off in his transference, the style of the worldly woman that the young girl observes in silence all through the party.

When Alfred Adler talks about a life-style as the way to grasp the nature of a person's neurosis, he is on to the truth that style shows how a person handles his feelings, how he gives feeling to the contents of consciousness, how his values are lived. As methodical order expresses thinking, so does style express feeling. As the style of a period expresses the modalities of feeling of an era, so the style of a person reveals his feeling life. When it does not change with the stages of life, the way historical periods change our modes of style, then style becomes caricature and stylization. The less observable the style (the less it is stylized), the more it is part of the way a person simply is, the more we can claim for him an integration of feeling, so that his feeling manner is indistinguishable from him. He is all of a piece, in keeping with his style. Thus, the development of one's own style in painting or writing is the highest goal of the artist as well as the mark which lasts the longest. For the rest of us the lesson is the same: the search to find ourselves is the search to find our style, the way to live feeling in life.

Tact, or the sense of timing, is perhaps the crown of appropriate feeling. Ecclesiastes puts it simply: to everything there is a season. Everything has its time. Perhaps feeling is merely tactfulness, a matter of timing. Humor depends wholly on it, and music is the art of time. The feeling function perceives time: as, for instance, when visiting a person in the hospital, staying not too short or too long, feeling the time to get up and go. The quality of time, rather than the amount one gives another, carries the feeling. For this reason, disturbed feeling —the guilty feelings from the mother-complex—distorts the time sense, and one gives quantities of time with only grains of feeling.

Time has a quality—or is a quality. It is not but an accumula-
tion of endlessly clicking identical minutes into eternity. The
development of the time sense means the development of feeling awareness of the moment and of biography different from
the moment constructed by the thinking clock. Rather there is a
moment as quantitatively long or short as feeling shapes it.
Moments have sizes: there are long moments, big moments, and
moments so crowded that nothing finds place. Feeling shapes
time, breaking it up into various kinds of feeling tones. These
tones are not on the same band of continuity as seven o'clock
follows six which followed five. Feeling time is organized in
clusters, more like an organic growth, so that today has its roots
perhaps in a day last summer (and not yesterday which belonged to a wholly different branch). Thus we do pick up old
relationships again where we left off. And thus is continuity so
essential for feeling development.

The elapse of time may or may not alter the feeling function.
When we hold a thing long and wrong, we still resent; but sometimes, through continuity, the feeling function finds a new connection and new value to an event and we can forgive. Again,
there is no other education possible but that of courage to bear
the long-drawn-out unchanging aspect of oneself. This teaches
the feeling function patience. How long to hold and when to let
go are again matters of timing; one has no better guide than the
"inner voices" of the feeling function and has to trust the guide.

We can also somewhat be guided by the *effects* we have on
others. We may not see ourselves, but we can watch another's
face, hear his voice, and tell something about the effect we are
having. The extraverted feeler can make the other person feel
good. He gives value, compliments, help; he smooths a friction
and notices a need. He can have an encouraging effect. And one
might look for these effects: What do we bring in the room with
us? What sounds through our voice besides the words we are
talking? How much fear do we evoke? Do we bring anyone ever
a laugh, or must they always be defending themselves, guilty?
Does time run by quickly or drag?

Feeling may be in essence only a matter of giving time to
things; and patience, or the art of slowness, may be, as mysticism
says, the final flower of human feeling. Beyond the fleetingness

of *anahata*-feeling, there is a slowness without depression and a lightness without inflation. When I have no time for you, I give you little value. And when we inquire to what a person gives his time, or to whom, we discover a great deal about his feeling. The time one spends may express the feeling itself being given.

These traditional forms of feeling education—manners, style, timing, personal relationships, marriage, feeling-fantasies, falling-in-love—show ways that have always been there. They show that feeling does not need specific programs for its education. I am sarcastic about the popular movement of *feeling-groups*, not because feeling does not need development, but because their starting-point is imposed upon life. They are techniques. They seem another form of community Protestantism, where one "works" at love of neighbor under the delusional enthusiasm of self-improvement. Sensitivity groups do not give enough room to the depressive recognition of the fixity of habits and the limits of love, personality and transformation. Besides, they emphasize the personal and momentary, whereas the feeling function needs prolonged continuity and relation to objective values and impersonal realities. We are mistaken in believing that these groups belong to Eros, for that God singles individuals out with his arrows and connects individuals into couples through intimacy, notoriously placing intimacy before community. Eros develops feeling through the faces of love: *pothos* (longing), *himeros* (desire), *anteros* (responding), *philia, agape, caritas*. It is not yet clear which God has called the groups into life, but we do know they began as therapy. They derive from a sick situation, and the feeling that develops there must be seen at least in part in terms of this origin, just as the feeling in analysis also reflects its background of psychopathology out of which analysis arose. We have groups now because the traditional forms of meeting—drinking, banqueting, whoring, fighting, mourning, plotting, dancing—have lost out and require substitutes. At least the groups offer a substitute where some pathology may be enacted; what education of the feeling function takes place there is yet to be seen.

There are many *psychopathologies* of feeling. In fact distortions of the feeling function, such as hysterical reactions or schizoid ambivalence, are main criteria of psychopathology in general.

Psychopathy, for instance, described as an absence of the moral sense, or "moral insanity," would seem to refer to peculiarities of the feeling function. These things are described in any text-book of abnormal psychology and psychiatry.

But there are other peculiarities which bear attention. For example, *avoidance*. There is a peculiar trait some of us show —ducking out of feeling. We use the classical New-England clamp-jawed "I should prefer not to talk about that" when something gets too close and personal. Or we take the feelings into a group, for a catharsis, excited by their discovery and their expression, yet avoiding their consequences.

Or we can turn to Eastern things, which beautifully avoids feeling development. Flower arrangement in the manner of the Japanese master or transcendental meditation have not much to do with the actualities of the feeling function. We might do more for its development by exploring the cultural formation of this function through study of Hawthorne, Hardy, Emerson, and John or Wesley (in the Protestant case), and spending some time in Kentucky or Kansas (or with our parents) than pilgrimaging to an ashram where the modes of feeling have nothing to do with our own. The Eastern path is a way around the differentiation of personal feeling, substituting for it collective gentleness and self-control. Another culture provides a backdrop for contrasting styles. Henry James shows the American style of feeling by placing it in Paris. So we read French literature or watch Italian films to feel more accurately our differences. To take on the foreign culture and its feeling style provides a collective formula—one now has a Buddhist name or wears a sari—but the education of the function is still avoided.

Usually we avoid feeling by turning it over to someone else: the other partner in the marriage, the best friend, the secretary or interior decorator or analyst who "guides" us, telling us how to go home and "relate" to the children. Sometimes we avoid by living it all inside with exaggerated introvertedness, never functioning with it outwardly in the life of people, values, and tastes; or the reverse: we live so feelingly outward that we avoid altogether the despair and mixups of our personal subjectivity.

We may recall that where feeling functions well a person will find importance given to his subjective and/or objective worlds.

The rest of us have trouble in recognizing what is important. We get dejected, or inflated, and our absent sense of what is significant harries us into the pursuit of happiness. We are content neither with ourselves nor with our situations. The feelers—even if anxious with ideas, abstractions, plans and dates—yet can be content, even stupidly smug, because their feeling gives value and importance to their psychic contents, relationships and circumstances. So, the feeling types tend to be more secure and to be less afflicted with urgent curiosity, rebellion and a need for change.

The division within the function between its extraverted and introverted faces may account for all those strange phenomena called *split feeling.* The inferior function goes underground. Then we lose access to many of our feelings; they disappear with the function. Then I do not know what I feel and cannot express a feeling without putting myself into a special sort of split condition. Rather than saying "I am a bitter, mean and dried man," or "I want you," or "I love sitting in this room," we put distance or time between what we feel and how we express it, saying "I used to feel that way," or "When I was a child I always wanted," or "Someday, when I am an old man I shall be loving and kind." We are not present where the feelings are, and where the feelings are we are not. We have split ourselves from them. When a woman asks a man after ten years of marriage: "Do you love me?" it is less her doubt (for she could not settle her doubt with any answer he might give), but rather an attempt to connect the man with his feelings. His answer forces him to feel what he feels, now, to be where his feelings are.

Split feeling shows in other forms. Some express feelings only through letters at a distance; vis-à-vis they are tongue-tied. Some only find their feeling after sitting alone in the dark, writing something down, playing the piano. Some must use another language, as the love scene in *The Magic Mountain* where Thomas Mann drops his native German and has the characters speak in French. Some find their love fantasies stirred only through travel posters of distant places, or a foreign mistress, or something to do with the future, or another century in the past when they would rather have lived. Feeling is always somewhere, sometime else: "not here," she says; "not now," he says.

Now at the end, I suppose the crucial test of courage concerns the psychopathologies of feeling, those aspects that cannot fit in with the fantasy of education. Parts never change and never will change, and completion means including the alchemical sludge that is merely sludge, the derelict wastage of one's incorrigible and unredeemed feeling weaknesses. Saturn too rules the soul, and his limits refuse the fantasy that everything is subject to development.

We have been subject to a kind of inferior feeling-philosophy that everything in human nature can be improved, or integrated, or made conscious. Over analysis there hangs an invisible sign saying "growth" (or "transformation"). By means of this optimistic feeling-philosophy we pay lip service to the feeling function. The vagueness of the idea suits the imprecision of inferior feeling (or inferior thinking of the feeling type), giving us a comfortable and harmonious notion that whatever happens is ultimately for the good, part of growth, part of the individuation process.

Yet we know from our own lives and watching the lives of others, especially those older, that we contain appalling gaps of unimproved feeling: hatreds that "should" have been over, shabbiness and cheapness, neglect at critical moments, leftover longings into old age, wounds unhealed, betrayals unadmitted, cruelties continually perpetrated. T. S. Eliot ("Little Gidding" of the *Four Quartets*, London, 1944) describes "the gifts reserved for age," one of which is ". . . the rending pain of re-enactment /Of all that you have done, and been; the shame/Of motives late revealed, and the awareness/Of things ill done and done to others' harm/Which once you took for exercise of virtue.'"

Although the painful psychopathologies remain to the end, we do have *friendships* as a place for these feelings. Friendship was considered in antiquity to be one of man's finest accomplishments, something rare and reserved for the latter part of life. Friendship does not exist under the invisible sign of transformation; friends are not out to improve each other, since they accept each other by putting up with each others' pathologies. Friendship offers a feeling context in which the shameful awareness of inferior feeling can be bared. The re-enactments of the past and the revelations of one's wounds can be ruminated upon. Even analysis does not offer pathology such a warm home as does friendship.

But friendship too remains on the level of personal feeling. The psyche has yet further needs for *impersonal* satisfaction. But until our culture has re-established a harmony with the major archetypal forces within life—the diurnal rhythms and the seasons, the markings of time in biography and the spirits of place, the ancestors, offspring, family and nation, the movements of historical events, and death—in terms of the Gods and Goddesses who govern the personal, our feeling function necessarily remains in one essential respect inferior, even pathological. For it is deprived by the secular world in which we are set from bearing the values of and connecting existence with archetypal reality.

BIBLIOGRAPHY
Literature for Further Reading

Chapter I

H. M. Gardiner, R. C. Metcalf, J. G. Beebe-Center, *Feeling and Emotion: A History of Theories* (New York, 1937).

Feelings and Emotions: The Wittenberg Symposium, ed. M. Reymert (Clark University, 1928).

Feelings and Emotions: The Mooseheart Symposium, ed. M. Reymert (New York: McGraw-Hill, 1950).

Feelings and Emotions: The Loyola Symposium, ed. M. B. Arnold (New York and London: Academic Press, 1970).

J. Hillman, *Emotion: A Comprehensive Phenomenology of Theories and Their Meanings for Therapy* (London and Evanston, 1960/64).

T. S. Eliot, *Four Quartets* (London, 1944).

Chapter II

Psychological Types, volume 6 of *The Collected Works*, contains all of Jung's writings on typology. *The Collected Works* are translated by R. F. C. Hull, edited by H. Read, M. Fordham, G. Adler, and Wm. McGuire, and published by Princeton University Press (Princeton, 1953 ff.) and in Great Britain by Routledge and Kegan Paul (London). References hereafter to the *CW* will be cited by volume (1–20) and paragraph numbers.

Chapter III

Journal of Analytical Psychology 13/1 (1968): papers by I. N. Marshall, by H. Mann, M. Siegler, H. Osmond, and by H. G. Richek and O. H. Brown.

Journal of Analytical Psychology 9/2 (1964): paper by K. Bradway.

There have been many and sometimes rather odd attempts to discover the feeling type in biography or in art, or to diagnose the feeling type through tests, or to equate the feeling function with specific styles. For some of this literature see: A. Aigrisse, *Psychanalyse de la Grèce antique* (Paris, 1960), who finds the Dionysian religion represents the feeling function (as the Olympian Gods stand for extraversion and Demeter for the sensation function); W. P. Witcutt, *Blake: A Psychological Study* (London, 1946), claims Blake for the introverted intuitives and remarks upon his feeling function; H. Read, *Education through Art* (London, 1943), discusses the kinds of drawing and painting feeling-type children characteristically produce. On diagnostic tests and the types, see the work of H. Gray and J. Wheelwright, and the Myers–Brigg Type Indicator (1962), available from the Educational Testing Services (Princeton, New Jersey). A survey of the literature and a validation of this type-testing can be found in L. J. Stricker and J. Ross, "An Assessment of Some Structural Properties of the Jungian Personality Typology," *Journal of Abnormal Social Psychology* 68 (1964): 62–71.

Chapter V

C. G. Jung, "Psychological Aspects of the Mother Archetype," in *CW* 9, i.

E. Neumann, *The Great Mother* (London, 1955).

M. E. Harding, *Woman's Mysteries* (Pantheon, 1955).

J. Hillman, "Friends and Enemies," *Harvest* 8 (1962): 1–22.

A. Guggenbühl-Craig, "Must Analysis Fail through Its Destructive Aspect?" *Spring 1970*: 133–45.

Chapter VI

C. G. Jung, "Anima and Animus," in *CW* 7; "The Syzygy: Anima and Animus," in *CW* 9, ii; "Concerning the Archetypes, with Special Reference to the Anima Concept," in *CW* 9, i; "An Account of the Transference Phenomena Based on the Illustrations to the 'Rosarium philosophorum,'" in *CW* 16.

Emma Jung, *Animus and Anima* (Spring Publications, 1957).

Frances Wickes, *The Inner World of Choice* (New York, 1963; third edition, Boston: Sigo Press, 1988), ch. 11, 12.

Linda Fierz-David, *The Dream of Poliphilo*, Bollingen Series (New York: Pantheon, 1950; reissued, Dallas: Spring Publications, 1987).

J. Hillman, *Insearch: Psychology and Religion* (New York: Charles Scribner's Sons, 1967; reissued, Dallas: Spring Publications, 1979), ch. 4.

E. C. Whitmont, *The Symbolic Quest* (New York: G. P. Putnam's Sons, 1969), ch. 12.

Books of Permanent Jungian Interest

Women's Dionysian Initiation • Linda Fierz-David

Rare Pompeiian fresco art depicting an initiation ceremony for women in a series of ten exquisite scenes provides the basic material for the author's psychological analysis. We feel the events of extraordinary life lived in the company of Dionysos from Ariadne's point of view. These ancient mysteries once enacted collectively continue today, according to M. Esther Harding's introduction, in "the secret recesses of the heart." Color plates. (149 pp.)

Eros on Crutches • Adolf Guggenbühl-Craig

An examination of psychopathy that evokes sympathy for the psychopath even as it explores his radical defects of character. The author reads psychopathy not so much as a moral flaw but as an absence of Eros. Includes chapters entitled "Outsiders, Delinquents—and Invalids of Eros," "Historical Development of the Term Psychopathy." An important contribution to precise diagnostics for the clinician and to reflection for the psyche. (126 pp.)

The Logos of the Soul • Evangelos Christou

Christou pushes the languages of science, philosophy, and art to their limit, demonstrating that only psychological reality creates the experience that is at the same time its object of study. One must be prepared for the conclusions of such insight: all psychology is psychotherapy; manifestation, not adaptation, measures therapeutic effectiveness; therapy with another is always self-therapy; self-therapy is inextricably world therapy. (iv, 104 pp.)

The Self in Psychotic Process • John Weir Perry

The author's therapy in the California Bay Area with acute episodes in young psychotic patients brought him national and international renown. The case of the young housewife diagnosed catatonic schizophrenic demonstrates the interpenetration of collective symbols and individual processes as they come to light in "breakdown" (Part One), and extends knowledge of the psyche by elucidating symbols of the Self (Part Two). This second edition includes a new preface by Dr. Perry, together with the original Foreword by C. G. Jung, scholarly apparatus, illustrations, and index. (xv, 184 pp.)

The Japanese Psyche • Hayao Kawai

Addresses such questions as why so few Japanese fairy tales end in a "happily-ever-after" marriage and why the female figure best expresses the culture's ego and the country's possible future. The author compares Japanese and Western tales, throwing into relief the former's idiosyncratic figures and themes. Terrible women who eat people, obscene escapes from the Oni (frightening but sometimes comic male demons), brother–sister bonds, undersea dragon palaces: with such elements does Kawai delicately present the multiple layers of the Japanese psyche. (234 pp.)

Spring Publications, Inc. • *P.O. Box 222069* • *Dallas, Texas 75222*

-eros - love directed
toward Self realization

-Contaminate - To make
unfit for use by untro
of unwholesome or un-
desireable elements